startups

uild a better business

BRIGHT
MARKETING
OR SMALL BUSINESS

KE YOUR BUSINESS STAND OUT FROM THE CROWD

To Cal, Jessie, Bonnie and Ben

startups build a better business

BRIGHT MARKETING FOR SMALL BUSINESS

MAKE YOUR BUSINESS STAND OUT FROM THE CROWD

ROBERT CRAVEN

crimson

Acknowledgements

A special thank you to everyone who made this book possible: Tricia, Ant, James and the team at The Directors' Centre; David and the team at Crimson; and of course, the 15,000 attendees at the *Bright Marketing* events.

Thank you.

Bright Marketing for Small Business

This edition published in Great Britain in 2011 by
Crimson Publishing
Westminster House
Kew Road
Richmond
Surrey
TW9 2NB

First published in 2007 as Bright Marketing
© Robert Craven 2011

A catalogue record for this book is available from the British library.

ISBN 978 1 85458 562 2

Typeset by Nicki Averill Design
Printed and bound in the UK by Ashford Colour Press, Gosport, Hants

CONTENTS

PART FOUR: A BRIGHT MARKETING MANIFESTO

FOREWORD

Most of us from time to time have been on the receiving end of poor marketing. Have you ever walked out of a shop because what you wanted was out of stock, or the queue was too long or the service poor? Have you ever complained and got an unsatisfactory response? Or changed a supplier because they didn't treat you like a valued customer?

We can all recognise poor marketing in others, but perhaps you've looked at your own marketing effort and wondered. Wondered why it isn't bringing in the results you want. Wondered exactly which 50% was wasted. Maybe you've wondered why prospects don't return your calls, or why you couldn't quite clinch that deal.

Maybe you've looked at some of the websites and textbooks by marketing experts and come away unsatisfied, thinking it was all too complicated, too expensive or simply not for you.

Perhaps you've had a look at the celebrity entrepreneurs who seem to hog the TV screens these days, and wish they'd come down from their multimillionaire ivory towers, and speak in your language?

Or maybe you simply don't know where to start.

Wherever you are on your business journey, this book is for you.

Robert Craven knows about business. A serial entrepreneur himself, he has delivered his *Bright Marketing* seminars to thousands of business people. They are lively, stimulating, even provocative – I know, I've attended them. Anyone who starts a seminar by advising you to 'sack 50% of your customers' is bound to attract your attention.

Starting at basic questions: 'Why should people bother to buy from you when they can buy from the competition?' and 'What makes your business different from the rest?', he puts in place all the building blocks to enable his audience to go away confident that they can make their marketing more effective and their business more profitable. They are entertained, they are involved, they participate.

Not everyone can attend his events – though they should – so in this book he has brought together all he has learned about marketing. No jargon, no theory – just simple and practical steps you can take to improve your sales and your profitability. It is presented in an easy and logical framework, with checklists and exercises to complete, and while it is the closest thing to attending his seminars in person, it is an entertaining read from end to end.

In the book Robert puts forward his rule of 'Seven By Three'. He reckons that in a world full of noise and competing demands for our attention, you need to repeat your message at least 21 times if it is to be remembered. And that, I think, is the key to getting the best out of this book. Don't read it once and put it on the shelf. Rather you should keep it handy to dip into regularly – perhaps when you have run up against a problem, or simply for a quiet five minutes over a coffee when you want to brush up on a topic.

Bright Marketing really can make a difference to your business.

George Derbyshire
Chief executive
National Federation of Enterprise Agencies

BRIGHT MARKETING!

Getting ahead of the competition

- Why should people bother to buy from you when they can buy from the competition?
- What makes your business different from the rest?

We live in a world where everything claims to be better and yet everything seems to be the same...
– *Bright Marketing* argues that in a world full of mediocrity it doesn't take that much to stand out from the competition. How do you do that?

Most businesses try to be all things to all people...
– they become seen as a jack-of-all-trades. On the other hand, the business that adopts the principles of *Bright Marketing* becomes known for its deep understanding/knowledge (and can charge premium prices!); it becomes recognised as the first port of call. The trick is to know how to make that happen.

In a world that celebrates celebrity, people have a choice...
– they can buy from the 'me too' also-rans, or they can buy from the market leaders. Whether you trade locally, regionally, nationally or internationally you can put yourself ahead of the competition.

Most businesses are only expert at the technical side of their job and they don't know how to communicate effectively with their customers...
– meanwhile, customers buy from the company that they believe will do the best job. So, the likelihood is that the customer will buy from the business that they, the customer, believe is the best. Is that you?

The real problem is that most businesses are too much in love with themselves and what they do...

– and they don't spend enough time looking at their businesses through the eyes of the customer.

You Need To Stand Out From The Rest, But How Do You Do That?

Bright Marketing will show you how to become seen in your field. The book is about branding... it is about positioning... it is about entrepreneurship... but actually it is about a whole lot more.

A Marketing Book For Professional Marketers?

Yes and no! Well, mainly no! *Bright Marketing* does not set out to be a standard marketing book or a textbook. It was not written with any exams or qualifications in mind. However, professional marketers will appreciate its down-to-earth approach to getting more sales; in fact, we go out of our way to focus on how a business can get more sales.

In reality we now have, and we welcome, a large following of professional marketers who consider themselves to be *Bright Marketers* applying the *BM* techniques to their workplace or to that of their clients.

So Is It For You?

If you run your own business and want a no-nonsense guide to getting more customers (with relatively little expenditure) then this is for you. If you are helping to grow a business then this is for you.

If you want practical tools to help you get more customers then this is for you!

So What Makes This Book Different From All The Other Marketing and Sales Books?

This book is not based on years of painstaking, but dull, methodical research... it is *not* based on some clever clogs theories that only marketing professors can understand.

This book is based on stuff that works for businesses like yours.

And The Workshops?

The book is based on the award-winning *Let's Talk... Bright Marketing* workshops, where we have asked over 15,000 business directors and owners to tell us what they wanted to know about marketing. What emerged was a seminar that gave the delegates the answers they wanted in a form that they could apply to their businesses that very day.

Do You Have To Attend The Workshop?

No. Absolutely not, but it would be great to see you at one.

The book is a free-standing volume that should be read independently of the workshops. You do not need to have attended one. The only prerequisite to reading the book is your enthusiasm and willingness to seek out better ways to help you to grow your business.

The most important thing to understand about the tools and techniques in the book is that they work; quite simply, you will make more profit if you apply the *Bright Marketing* ideas. We've used them ourselves in our own businesses as well as in those of our clients; we've got stacks of testimonials and references to prove that our advice and materials will help you to get more customers and to get more profitable customers.

To find out more about the *Bright Marketing* seminars and workshops, visit www.bright-marketing.com

How Does This Fit With Robert's Other Books?

Bright Marketing shares my no-nonsense approach to business that was encapsulated in *Kick-Start Your Business* and in *Customer Is King*.

Use the Website

A website has been set up, www.bright-marketing.com, to work alongside the book. The website contains guides, articles, case studies and materials to support you in your quest to get more (and more profitable) customers and clients for your business. It also contains free bonus materials for readers of the book. The password is 'bright'.

The Structure of the Book

Bright Marketing is divided into four parts.

1. **First Steps** We begin by examining the heart of what marketing is (or rather isn't) and what it means to you.

2. **What Works – Tools For All** These are the tools that get used by nearly every business we work with – tools that you can't afford to miss.

3. **Other Tools – Help Yourself** A selection of tools, some of which you will find incredibly useful to help you to grow your business (while some may not be so appropriate for your particular business!).

4. **A Bright Marketing Manifesto** We bring together the *BM* 'ology' in a series of Laws, Crunch Questions, and the Manifesto itself.

Use The Book

Use the book however *you* want.

Read it from start to finish.

Or just go straight to the techniques that you need for your business.

Scribble in the margin, underline things you want to remember – my only plea is that you do use the book as a lever to improve your business.

Your business will not change unless you act – action is at the heart of this book. I can only show you the tools to use; *you* must use them.

The mere fact that you feel driven to buy the book suggests that you want to make some changes.

'Go For It!'

Robert Craven
rc@robertcraven.co.uk
Bath, May 2011

PART ONE: FIRST STEPS

FIRST STEPS

- The FAQs Of Marketing
- What Is Marketing?
- Why Should People Bother To Buy From You?
- What Is Your Marketing Strategy?
- Why Doesn't (Traditional) Marketing Work?
- Marketing Effectiveness: How Good Is My Marketing?
- How Am I Doing? How Good Is My Marketing?

We begin by examining the heart of what marketing is (or rather isn't) and what it means to you. Delegates at our workshops keep asking the same basic questions about marketing, the FAQs. Maybe we should call them the VFAQs (Very Frequently Asked Questions).

We list the key questions and go on to consider what marketing is, why it doesn't (usually) work, and how good you might be at it.

The purpose of Part One is to cover the basic ground, the fundamentals that underpin the *Bright Marketing* Manifesto.

THE FAQS OF MARKETING

The first *Bright Marketing* seminar took place in mid-2002 and since then the workshop has been delivered over 200 times to approximately 15,000 business owners, managers and directors. Why had they come? What did they want to know?

Every event has started the same way, asking the question,

'By the end of this session, what do you want to know how to do?'

Having asked the question over two hundred times we now have a pretty good idea of the key marketing issues that people want sorted. This book has encapsulated the key questions (and more importantly the answers!) in a digestible format; use it how you see fit.

At its simplest, the main themes that the audiences wanted to know the answers to came under one of seven headings:

- What works?
- How to communicate? How to get heard?
- How to focus? How to target?
- How to measure?
- How to stand out from the rest/how to be listened to?
- How to get more sales with no budget?
- How to make it happen?

What you will notice in the chapters of this book is that nothing fits neatly into one heading – most overlap. As a result I have written chapters in the natural order that subjects were dealt with in the actual workshops.

In the 200 events we spoke to MDs of multinationals as well as owner-managers of smaller businesses and the same themes just kept coming through to us.

To give you a rough idea of the top questions, they were as follows:

- How do I get into bigger businesses?
- What works best?
- What do people buy?
- How can I make people buy from us?
- How do you get the 'biggest bang for your buck'?
- How do we know how we are doing?
- How can we make more money?
- How much should we invest in marketing?
- If there was only one thing we could do then what should it be?
- How can I sell more?
- How can I get more customers?
- How can I get more profitable customers?
- How can I get my team to understand the marketing plan?

So what? What's next?

This book will show you the answers to these questions – in other words, how to get more (and better) clients to buy from you.

WHAT IS MARKETING?

Marketing, to me, is one of those misunderstood words of the business world. Like 'strategy', we use the word 'marketing' all over the place and give it different meanings depending upon our mood and our inclination. No wonder no-one respects these words or the people who use them a lot.

A Textbook Definition (unhelpful and dull!)

The textbook definition of marketing is

'identifying and satisfying customer needs profitably'

... but this is a very dry and academic definition and not very helpful if you are running a business.

Slightly Better

A better definition might be

'Marketing is about deciding what customers' business you want to win... against whom... and how.'

So, At Its Core We Can Say...

'Marketing is seeing your business through your customers' eyes.'

Ask Yourself

■ What problem does our product or service solve?

....
....
....

■ Why should people buy from us?

....
....
....

■ What benefits are we offering that our competition doesn't offer?

....
....
....

■ If we aren't offering additional benefits then why should people buy from us at all?

....
....
....

Key Point

Your business leaks messages about itself like radioactivity. It is not possible to not communicate – you always communicate; everything you do communicates something. So, you should decide what it is that you wish to be communicating, be clear about who you want to be communicating with… and what the message is that you want them to receive.

In some senses, marketing equals communication.

Another, Broader, Definition (sounds dull but does the job)…

'Marketing is about systematically selecting how and what you communicate to whom… with the purpose of winning more of the business that you want.'

Regis McKenna…
'Marketing is everything.'

So What?

I hear you wondering. Well, if most people don't know or can't agree about what marketing is, then why should we be surprised if most people are so poor at it! So, yes, marketing is everything, and yes, marketing is about systematically selecting how and what you communicate to whom... with the purpose of winning more of the business that you want'.

WHY SHOULD PEOPLE BOTHER TO BUY FROM YOU? (WSPB2BFY?)

At the heart of the *Bright Marketing* Manifesto is the one-liner 'Why should people bother to buy from you when they can buy from the competition?'. This sentiment haunts and underpins the whole book.

Stop and Think

Why should people bother to buy from you if you are the same as the competition?

Sorry, I can't think of a single reason! And I certainly can't think of a single reason in a world where your competition is...
Cheaper
Or faster
Or friendlier
Or higher tech
Or whatever!

The Big Question

In fact, this is the big question for banks, building societies, shops, consultants, pubs, almost any business... Why should people bother to buy from you? 'WSPB2BFY?'

If you can't answer this question then 'do not pass go, do not collect £200'.

Stop and Think

We live in a world of mediocrity – everything claims to be better but actually everything is the same.

We employ...

Similar people with...
Similar qualifications at...
Similar salaries to use...
Similar software on...
Similar machines to deal with...

Similar customers with similar needs so that we can sell them…
Similar products at…
Similar prices to those of our…
Similar competitors!

Key Point

In this world of similarity and mediocrity, we only need to be 5% different from the competition to stand out!

Fact

Please memorise and inwardly digest the following:

The only products that succeed are those that offer a benefit to consumers…
…that is greater than their cost.

Fact

I know that this is obvious… but often we are in the business of (re-)stating the obvious…

People normally buy benefits and not features.

A key problem (particularly for business owners) is that we get so pre-occupied with the features that we have given our product, we forget why the customer might wish to buy it in the first place!

Be Different Now

I love this quote from Seth Godin…

'Professional service marketing is certainly among the safest I've seen. Because it appears to take no risks, it's actually quite risky.'

You risk more by obsessing with safety in numbers, by being unremarkable. On your gravestone they can write:

'Here lies another businessman
His business did OK, but not great
No-one will remember him that well
But at least he looked like everyone else.'

Some Further Thoughts: What Do People Really Buy?

We are all customers and consumers – we all go out and buy products and services for our homes and for our businesses so it feels bizarre to have to go back to the basics of business and ask 'What do people really buy?'.

So What?

Do you offer a benefit to your consumer that is greater than the cost?

WHAT IS YOUR MARKETING STRATEGY?

If 'marketing is everything', and 'marketing is about systematically selecting how and what you communicate to whom... with the purpose of winning more of the business that you want' then how do you do it?

A good starting point, ironically is your end point. If you know what 'success' looks like then it is much easier to plan a route to get 'there'.

Like any other strategy (another over-used word!), your strategy for marketing is your route map for getting there. The fundamental question, then, is 'what is your marketing vision?' Write it down. In other words:

Why... which customers... will choose us?

Action Point: Your Marketing Vision

Write down:

1. **Your market position (how you compare with the competition) now, and in the future.** [eg now we are Number 10 restaurant in the town; in three years we will be Number Two by turnover]

....
....
....
....
....

2. **Your customer position (how they see you) now, and in the future.** [eg now we are the only modern funky place in the town, a bit too avant-garde; in three years we will be 'the place to eat']

....
....
....
....
....

3. How will you achieve and sustain this new position?
[eg delivering a consistent and remarkable customer experience combined with encouraging word-of-mouth and referral/recommendations – creating a real buzz]

....
....
....
....
....

In any business you are trying to create a product offering, or more specifically a brand.

A Brand Is...

A brand can be defined as a combination of the following:
- Signs by which you are known and remembered
- A bundle of explicit/implicit promises
- A reflection of personality
- A statement of position.

And... by the time you finish this book, you should have sorted out how and what your brand should be communicating and to whom.

WHY DOESN'T (TRADITIONAL) MARKETING WORK?

Marketing and marketers are quite rightly under attack. Put simply, traditional marketing behaves like the emperor's new clothes – everyone points and marvels at how wonderful it is. At the same time, we seem to invest a lot of time and money in marketing, but without getting the promised returns.

Five Reasons Why 'Normal Marketing' Fails (Especially For Your Business)

We can fire bullets at the 'Marketing Establishment' until the cows come home. This will not help your business very much. So, let's be specific about the main reasons why marketing fails in your business. The list is simple.

1) Lack Of Commitment

If you don't really believe in your product, or if you are not consistent and regular in the ways that you promote it, then the odds are that you will not succeed. Your plans must ensure that you have committed the appropriate resources and effort to do what it takes to make your product sell.

2) Lack Of A Clear Benefit

You must sell something that people want. So, you have to get close to your customer (or potential customer) and find out what they really want, and examine what it is that you have to offer. Please don't make things just because you find them easy or fun to make. Customers do not care about how much fun you've had. They want to know WIIFM (*'What's In It For Me?'*).

3) Poor Positioning

If you look exactly the same as your competitors, and you offer the same benefits at the same price, then why should customers bother to buy from you? You need clarity about what it is that you offer and why customers should come to you. This, in turn, will inform you as to how to effectively promote and present yourself.

4) KISS

'Keep It Simple Stupid'! We have an ability to complicate things without realising that simplicity, clarity, and focus will bring us the profits we seek.

5) Paralysis By Analysis Combined With Dull Thinking

This is normally brought on by attending too many inappropriate marketing courses and reading too many textbooks aimed at professional marketing departments of large companies (where they can afford to be mediocre)!

Traditional marketing doesn't work so well nowadays because it is a crude and out-of-date way of behaving. In the old days there was a direct correlation between advertising spend and increases in sales. This is no longer the case.

Returns on advertising are falling as a result of simple supply and demand. Too many products are chasing the attention of time-poor, low-attention consumers through an ever-increasing number of media. The sums just don't add up anymore.

Key Point

Trading on the old tag lines no longer works. If all your competitors are competing on the strength of the usual banners (faster, smarter, better value) then why should people bother to buy from you if you are all just the same?

Now is the time to look at your business and try to make it look different on at least one significant criterion.

One-Liner

If there is a choice between being different and being better, then I'd rather be different. Ideally, I'd rather be different and the best!

What's To Be Done?

Look at your business through the eyes of the customer. Why should they buy from you? It does actually make sense to separate yourself from the masses rather than run with them.

Are You A Zebra?

Zebras that don't 'run with the pack' get noticed first – all the members of the herd of zebras look the same... and safe... when they are running in the herd. If you want to get noticed, try running 'outside the pack'. In the business world you are more likely to get noticed and this increases your chances of making a sale.

Homer Simpson on this very subject

'You know those balls that they put on car antennas so you can find them in the parking lot? Those should be on every car!'

And in Practice

Jay Abraham in the book *Guerrilla Marketing For Consultants* discusses how most management consultants promote themselves. All their (nigh-on identical) websites are at pains to demonstrate that they:

- Offer value for money, the best price
- Deliver contracts on time using recognised methods and approaches
- Employ well-qualified people, good credentials, experienced
- Are systematic
- Have a history of important clients
- Have exuberant but anonymous testimonials.

Key Point

In most industries there is too much sameness; too much safe differentiation between the various competitors. Often there is an over-supply of participants, as in the management consultancy industry, where the barriers to entry are also relatively low.

However, you might stand out as different in the mind of the customer if you have promoted something different, say, one of the following characteristics:

- A thought leader, a category authority, a prominent public speaking profile

Fact

You will be the same as the rest if you also try to attract work by celebrating qualities that are the same as your competitors'.

- A published expert, a new-wave thinker
- A list of testimonials from recognised characters
- A real guarantee (money back or payment on results only)
- True innovation or defying conventional wisdom, or even honesty.

Interruption Marketing!?

Traditional marketing can be seen as 'interruption' marketing. An attempt is made to present your own product to the consumer when their attention is high (and when they are most vulnerable to your message). Trains, cinema, TV and newspaper advertising see effectiveness plummeting as the target audiences become immune to more and more adverts that sell more and more products that seem pretty similar to the rest.

To survive in today's marketplace, you need to do more than simply copy the competition. That is a recipe for mediocre performance. You won't be remembered as you slip amongst the blur of mediocre providers all providing a 'much of a muchness'. You have been warned.

Stop and Think

In the old days, you knew when you were the target of an advertising campaign. Progressively the line between explicit advertising and more subtle promotion has become blurred. 'Product positioning' (buying the rights to a product being used in a high profile film or TV series) is a more and more common tactic to get one's product associated with the good and the worthy. Some 'unscrupulous' marketers even pay actors to conspicuously use and discuss a product in public places to generate a debate and interest.

It is time to figure out how to look different from the rest rather than the same as the rest. This is not about creating cheap gimmicks but it is about offering the clients and customers something that they value and can relate to.

MARKETING EFFECTIVENESS: HOW GOOD IS MY MARKETING?

In the *BM* workshops we use the worksheet below with clients to get them to think through just how good their marketing effectiveness is.

People regularly score their marketing on how much they have spent on it or how pretty their brochures look, ie marketing inputs or costs. These criteria seem somewhat superfluous. The very purpose of your marketing is to get more clients to buy from you... or to get your existing clients to stay with you and buy more. So what you really need to do is measure your marketing effectiveness (and not the inputs or costs).

Key Point

When evaluating your marketing, please measure its effectiveness – does it deliver the results that you want? Do not confuse the sizzle with the steak. Measure outputs and results.

Marketing is not an exercise in creating beautifully crafted works of art (unless that will get you more business!). Marketing is not an intellectually attractive process for stimulating the sensory sensitivities of an artistic director.

Marketing is all about communicating with potential/existing clients and getting them to buy from you rather than from your competitors. With that in mind, please score yourself on the worksheet on the next page.

Talk to almost any businessperson that has just come out of a standard marketing seminar. They resent the intellectually fascinating but unearthed, disconnected way that the subject relates to real actions.

Fact

Marketing, as it is commonly presented, is failing to deliver.

Your Marketing Effectiveness

1. We are totally committed to our marketing and sales plans.
   (if we have them in the first place!)

					%					
1 –	10 –	20 –	30 –	40 –	50 –	60 –	70 –	80 –	90 –	100
In your dreams					On a good day					Got it!

2. Customers know exactly what they get if they come to us!

3. Customers know why we are different from the rest.

4. We make everything simple and easy to understand for our customers *and* for ourselves.

5. Decision-making is easy because we are clear about what we are trying to do.

So What?

As most smart-assed marketing books claim, a new paradigm (read 'rhetoric') is required. Well, certainly a way of looking at finding and satisfying customers that is simple, yet effective, is required!

Problems with Sales and Marketing

You can figure out the help that people seek when you hear the kind of comments that they make when talking about marketing. The following are pretty standard comments; put ticks against the comments that you have muttered yourself at some point in the last few months!

- ■ 'Our pricing is easily matched/bettered by our competitors who seem to surpass and outflank us…'
- ■ 'Advertising is getting more expensive and less effective; too much time and money is spent on sales promotion and we don't know how effective it is…'
- ■ 'We're in the wrong business – maybe we should be a web designer 'cos they seem to be making all the money…'

- 'Sales force costs are rising…'
- 'Our so-called innovative projects often don't look much different from those of our competitors…'
- 'A lot is being given away…'
- 'We don't have a clear view of the future…'

It's time to take action.

You need to see marketing like any other business investment. Evaluate the cost and the subsequent benefit, that is, measure and evaluate inputs and outputs so that you establish what works most effectively for you.

HOW AM I DOING?

Before you can talk about what you wish to become, you need to have a clear idea of where you are now... and what your potential to grow, your capability, is like.

Using something like the 'FiMO' framework, defined below, you can identify strengths and weaknesses in the business and assess your capability to grow. This framework has now been applied to thousands of businesses with staggering results. It really tells you where you need to concentrate your efforts. And if you lie to it, you are simply cheating yourself.

Introduction

When you look at *your* own business, you need to somehow evaluate what is really going on. A framework is required to assist you to evaluate your performance (to date). There are plenty of business frameworks and models available from consultants and business schools. The trouble with them is that they do not always help you to create a better business.

This chapter introduces a framework that looks primarily at the business itself. This framework is referred to by the acronym *FiMO*.

FiMO is a framework for looking at your business and its performance. It can be used:
- By bankers to evaluate businesses
- By coaches and consultants working with businesses
- To write up business health checks
- To evaluate the strengths and weaknesses of your business
- To open up discussion within/with a company to discuss/ agree the 'state of play'.

Only a few businesses have some kind of plan or idea about what they are trying to do, and before you can look at future plans, you need to know how the business is performing right now.

Measuring Your Company's Performance To Date

When business people are asked

'What measures should be used to assess your company's performance to date?'

then the same list of answers is usually put forward, give or take one or two differences.

The list offered includes measures such as:
- Turnover in units and pounds
- Gross and net profit margin
- Return on capital employed
- Directors' salaries/owners' drawings
- Liquidity
- Cash-flow
- Stock
- Wages bill, and so forth.

While these financial measures are commendable as a list, to some degree they miss the point. What really matters is far more than just the financials.

Paul, the accountant, would come out with a statement like:

'Finance is the engine of the business without which there would be no reason for the company being in existence. Cash-flow is the oil that makes the business work, and therefore finance is the only thing that really matters.'

But still I feel drawn to say,

'To say that finance is the only thing that really matters is poppycock! There's more to understanding the business' performance than simply the financials. While I don't dispute the importance of finance, you need to recognise that it is simply a consequence of two other factors, marketing and operations...'

So, why do we always go to the financials when asked to evaluate performance to date?

There are several reasons.

One reason is that financials are easy to read and to measure – they somehow give a scientific and objective feel, after all the numbers can be compared and contrasted.

The second reason is that most business textbooks and studies look at a specific part or function of the business, for instance, marketing or finance. This approach makes study (and analysis) easier. Unfortunately the resultant output does not accurately reflect the reality of trying to run a real business.

The third reason lies with how businesses have received their teachings to date. Businesses get their 'knowledge' from a limited number of sources. Unfortunately, the knowledge that is shared with them is often based on theory and academic models rather than experience and easily applicable tools to really assist you.

For advice about running businesses, the traditional sources of help have been the accountants and the business support agencies, as well as the banks and universities, who usually have whole departments specialising in the use and application of financial measures to businesses. Up until recently it is almost as if a conspiracy by these parties has misled business people to think and believe that the financials are the only thing that really counts.

Key Point

A more accurate understanding of the business' performance to date is to recognise that financials only reflect the marketing and operations performance in the business. Financials are a consequence of marketing and operations performance.

Introducing The *FiMO* Framework For Looking At 'Performance To Date'

The framework we use to assess a company's performance to date is known as *FiMO*.

FiMO stands for:

Finance (Fi)
Marketing (M)
Operations and Production (O)

The *FiMO* framework gives a 'holistic' view of the business.

> ## Key Point
>
> A specialist in marketing will look for and see marketing issues as the key to a business situation; and an accountant will look for and see the financial issues. The *FiMO* framework gives us a much more balanced view of how the business has performed.
>
> So, you need to recognise that we have three interlocking and overlapping functions, both co-existing and interdependent. The image to be held in mind is that of a juggler – when all the balls move smoothly then there are no problems, but if one ball starts to misbehave then chaos ensues.

What We Mean By *Marketing* And *Operations* In This Context

Marketing is all about getting potential customers and selling to them. And there are as many measures of *marketing* as there are measures of *finance*.

Operations is all about producing the service or product. It is all about 'doing'. And there are as many measures of *operations* as there are of finance.

Most people that run their own business are preoccupied with the *making* and the *selling*. In other words, *operations* and *marketing*. In fact, most business owners are preoccupied with the *O* and the *M*, but don't know how to do marketing properly and effectively, so they put their effort into the *operations* while they have sleepless nights about how they could get more, better customers (*marketing*).

Without the ability to find customers and sell to them (the *marketing*), and the actual production or delivery of the service or product (the *operations*), then there would be very little to measure in terms of *finance*!

Action Point

Right now, score your business! Take each heading, and give your business a score out of 10 (where 0 is a very low score and 10 is a very high score).

How do the scores work?
- Scores of *2 or 3* suggest that there is something seriously wrong
- Scores of *4 or 5 or 6* suggest mediocrity
- Scores of *8 or 9* suggest that you are pretty good if not 'world class'. You might need to find some evidence to support your case. I would always question and challenge such scores.

In fact, write down the scores in the book, right here, on the page. After all this is a working book not a precious book to be kept clean. In fact, mark any pages in the book that you find of value.

So, here goes… mark your scores out of 10. Remember that this scoring system is subjective; it should be your gut response. By definition, this process is a little ambiguous and that is because we are interested in the process, the discussion, about what the scores mean and how they can be improved.

Heading:	Your score:
Finance	eg 6 ....
Marketing	eg 7 ....
Operations	eg 5 ....

As soon as you enter a number, you (or your colleagues) can argue why the score given was either too high or too low.

For instance, if you give yourselves 7 for finance:
- Why haven't you given yourself 8 or 6?
- What would you need to do to improve the score?

■ What makes you so sure that you only get a 7?
■ Is it 7 and improving, 7 and getting worse, or just stuck at 7?

This is a real process.
■ How can you justify your scores?
■ Where is the evidence?
■ What would you need to do to improve your score?
■ Why has your score not been better in the past?
■ Why haven't you sorted the underlying issues before?
■ Are you really sure that you are measuring appropriately?
■ Are you sure that you are measuring effectiveness
   (financial, marketing and operations effectiveness)
   rather than inputs or the activity?

Such a way of scoring immediately suggests how there might
be room for improvement.

   If you have filled in the *FiMO* scores for your business
then you can see how it gets you to think through and justify
the scores you have given. Try talking this through with a
colleague. How would they score your business under the
FiMO headings?

The figure below fleshes out some of the components under
each heading.

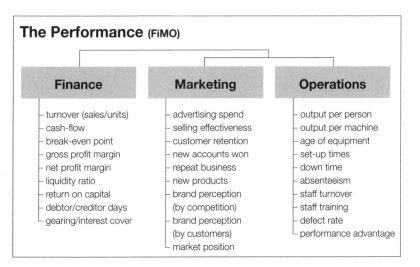

The Performance (FiMO)

Finance	Marketing	Operations
– turnover (sales/units)	– advertising spend	– output per person
– cash-flow	– selling effectiveness	– output per machine
– break-even point	– customer retention	– age of equipment
– gross profit margin	– new accounts won	– set-up times
– net profit margin	– repeat business	– down time
– liquidity ratio	– new products	– absenteeism
– return on capital	– brand perception	– staff turnover
– debtor/creditor days	(by competition)	– staff training
– gearing/interest cover	– brand perception	– defect rate
	(by customers)	– performance advantage
	– market position	

So What?

The *FiMO* framework shows you how your business performs. More importantly, it shows you how your financial performance is dependent on your *marketing* and *operations* performance. Finance is usually an average of your *marketing* and *operations* functions, so any improvement in either area will be seen in an improvement in your finance score – this is a good thing!

Most businesses we meet at the *Bright Marketing* seminars (over 90%!) score their *operations* performance at 6 or above but score their *marketing* at 5 or less.

In Conclusion

Two morals here. First, you need to know your 'performance to date' ('where are we now?') to establish your journey and direction. Second, in order to sort your financial performance, you must sort your marketing performance first.

__Part One: First Steps__ reminds us why getting your marketing/selling activities in order is a key priority. More importantly, it will be Bright Marketing *techniques (rather than the dull contents of so many marketing textbooks) that will move our businesses forward.*

__Next, Part Two: What Works: Tools For All__ shows you how to use the key tools in the Bright Marketing *toolkit – these are the ones that most businesses will use to improve their sales and profit performance.*

PART TWO: WHAT WORKS – TOOLS FOR ALL

WHAT WORKS

Part Two features the tools that get used by nearly every business we work with – tools that you can't afford to miss:

- Seven By Three (7x3)
- Identifying the Most Effective Sales Method
- The One-Minute Intro
- One-Minute Brand Test
- Asking For The Business – Three Versions
- The 80:20 Rule – The Law Of The Vital Few For Your Business
- Put Up Prices
- The Expert
- Put It All Together – The 'Customer Is King' Seven-Point Plan
- Customer Experience
- The Best-Kept Secret About Customer Service

By the time you have been through this section you will have covered the answers to the FAQs in chapter *The FAQs of Marketing*. The real skill is in incorporating the appropriate mix of these tools to help your business to improve its marketing and sales performance so that you run a better and more profitable business.

SEVEN BY THREE (7x3)

In a world of communication overload your message gets lost amongst all the others; you need to repeat your message many times before it is heard and remembered.

So What?

By midday of any particular day, we have typically seen or heard some 4,000 marketing messages – in newspapers and magazines, on cartons and packages, on the television and radio. Is it any wonder that most of our marketing activity seems to fail?

Fact

Today's marketplace is no longer responsive to the strategies that worked in the past.

Ries and Trout Said It

'There are too many products, too many companies, and too much marketing noise.'

So How Do You Get Heard In The Midst Of The Noise?

Repetition is the answer and the 'Rule Of Seven By Three' (which also happens to be my birthday!). We need to hear a message, on average, seven times to remember it! And only one in three messages actually reaches the target (spam-filters block them, dogs eat them, the postman loses them, the secretary bins them…)

You need to repeat your message at least 21 times if you want it to be seen or heard or more importantly if it is to be remembered. Most business people give up communicating long before that! And that's why your one-week radio ad, your mailshot, or your newspaper ads seem to fail to work – you just don't do it for long enough. Sobering stuff.

And in Practice

I've talked to all the major networking organisations (BNI, BRE, NRG) about how long it takes for new members to start making a profit from their networking activities. All the organisations agree that it takes roughly five months of attending weekly meetings for the new member's marketing message to get successfully communicated to the others. In other words, the message is put out about 20 times before the other networkers 'get it'. Confirmation of the Rule of Seven By Three – it takes roughly 21 times for people to actually hear your message.

How often have you actually kept plugging away at a marketing activity or campaign so that you've actually hit the target some 21 times...?

What would happen if you did?

IDENTIFYING THE MOST EFFECTIVE SALES METHOD

If you knew what the most effective sales method was then you would use it above others. The problem is that most people don't know what the most cost-effective sales method is so they don't know which one to use.

The Directors' Centre carried out a simple qualitative survey in Quarter One of 2004 (and repeated it in the first quarter of 2007). We asked one question:

'If you could only use one sales method then what would it be?'

The survey comprised a combination of questionnaires, surveys and interviews with a total of 247 directors and owner-managers from a cross-section of organisations of less than 200 employees. The style of the report was informal and not highly scientific to satisfy specific client needs – originally to 'confirm or refute findings and research found elsewhere'.

When asked what was 'the most effective sales method'… small and growing businesses put

- Face-to-face selling, and
- Referrals and customer recommendations

at the top of the list at Number One and Number Two.

Sales representatives from larger businesses also supported these survey findings – price was not the single most compelling sales feature, although clearly a low, competitive price can help. No, the success of most sales relationships was the result of relationships and reputation – face-to-face relationships which support the corporate brand communications spread by word-of-mouth – as the old adage goes, 'people buy from people'.

What Was Stopping Some Businesses From Being More Effective At Selling?

The answer came back as a lack of systems that 'test, review and improve' existing sales methods.

Some businesses try to sell things that the customer doesn't want!

Stop And Think

If you can't sell your product then it is for one of two reasons… either you've got a rubbish product, or you are rubbish at marketing and selling.

And the key question, to my mind, is:

'Can all businesses improve their sales performance by improving their sales skills, systems and techniques…?'

I think so!

A number of respondents commented on the artificial nature of the question ('If you could only use one sales method, what would it be?') and that the most powerful sales method was actually a combination of two or three techniques, eg exhibitions and face-to-face selling and telesales. And we agree with them here as well.

Our purpose was a 'finger in the air' response rather than an in-depth academic study. And now we use the table below as a starting point, a springboard, to get businesses to think about how they can improve their sales performance.

The Point is…

There are entire industries trying to sell us the least effective sales tools (email marketing, direct mail, exhibitions) while there are no formal industries trying to sell the most effective methods (face-to-face and recommendation). We believe their hype and they keep us ignorant of the fact that the cheapest solutions are the most effective for most people!

The results of the survey suggest a number of questions:

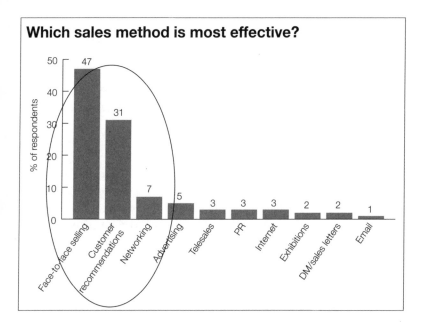

- Do you know which sales methods are the most effective in your business?
- Do you allocate sales effort in the most effective manner?
- Do you know how much it costs to acquire one new client?
- Do you know the average lifetime value of a new client?
- How much is the average new customer worth to you?

- If the 80/20 rule exists in your business (20% of efforts generate 80% of profits) then is this true for sales methods (ie 20% of sales methods generate 80% of sales)? What are you doing about it?
  - Do you know who the Top 20% of clients are? Do you treat them differently? Do you know what makes them different from the rest? Is there a way you could find more clients like them?
  - Are you trying to get more revenue from poor-performing clients, the 'trivial many'? (seems like hard work)… or are you trying to get more revenue from high-performing clients, the 'vital few'? (seems much easier to do)
  - Should you sack 50% of your 'poor' customers and get more (ie better) business from your 'richer' clients?

■ Has every part of your sales pipeline/system been measured, tested and systematised? If not, why not?

Most businesses interviewed believed that they were sales or customer-focused, but in reality, they spent little of their time systematically reviewing and improving their sales system(s).

Can We Do Better?

Most respondents (85%) agreed that better selling skills and behaviour were necessary to move their organisation forward. The key issue is whether the organisations (and individuals) are prepared to pay the price for such activity (ie make the changes required).

Barriers to Being More Effective at Selling

In a nutshell, key barriers are:
■ Lack of time, appropriate systems, tools, techniques, or even a complete absence of them!
■ Initiative fatigue – some staff are tired of being put through yet another business initiative which is supposed to transform their business
■ Lack of desire to make it happen
■ A feeling that selling is somehow 'dirty'.

Enablers to Becoming More Effective at Selling

For effective selling to become a fundamental part of how things are done, there needs to be a belief that better selling techniques will boost sales to the right sort of customers. We expect some combination of the following to be present to precipitate successful selling behaviour:
■ Appropriate skills/training, tested measurement and delivery systems
■ Attitude – A 'can do...', 'yes', and..., 'blame-free' culture that recognises that success and failure go hand-in-hand – a 'willingness to pay the price'
■ Rewards and systems that motivate the individuals concerned
■ Employing the right people, adopting the right strategy, and putting it all together so that it really works.

Selling And Training – Can Selling Be Taught?

Certainly, businesses (and individuals) can be coached, nurtured, coaxed and developed to become more selling-aware. What surprised us in the process of gathering the data was that even those who believe that selling is a crucial quality have done little (or nothing) to systematically assess or nurture positive attitudes towards the craft... or to really understand the needs and behaviour of their target customers.

So...

The following exercise gets you to start to measure and evaluate your marketing investment/performance. You start to put numbers to your marketing activity (costs, inputs, outputs, benefits); you start to test, monitor, track and evaluate your different options.

Action Point

Ask yourself these questions:

■ Where do you spend your marketing/sales time and money at the moment?
[eg 80% of time and money spent in conferences and exhibitions]

....
....
....
....
....

■ Where do you get your best results?
[eg referrals and recommendations]

....
....
....
....
....

■ Where should you spend your time and money?
[eg referrals and recommendations}

....
....
....
....
....

■ What could good marketing and selling skills do for your
business?
[eg an improvement of 10% in sales]

....
....
....
....
....

■ So, what are you going to do about it?

....
....
....
....
....

And in Practice

A substantial, nationwide accountancy practice invested over 10% of
turnover in marketing in its 'Year of The New Customer' in a bid to
gain more and better clients but to no avail. Despite an impressive
looking new website, flashy emails, a significant investment in telesales
and a very sexy brochure as well as a series of newspaper and TV
advertisements, there had been little noticeable improvement in
the number of new clients signed up. In fact, the new clients they
were getting weren't actually the type of clients that they had been
targeting! Time for a re-think.

After three months with little real success, the managing partner
announced the launch of 'Operation About Face' – a new initiative
with the sole aim of getting all staff out of the office to meet and
talk to as many prospective clients as possible; the real emphasis

was on getting to the face-to-face meeting and getting referrals and recommendations. 'Operation Referral' was also set up and every current client was asked for at least one referral. The impact of this activity saw new client acquisition rise by 200% – and the cost of new client acquisition fell from £1,000 to £350.

The new initiative was faster, cheaper and more effective than the traditional ways of marketing to new clients. As a postscript, it should be noted that they also did a fair amount of work polishing up the way that they presented themselves and the business.

See also: Chapter on *One-Minute Intro* on *Asking for the Business.*

Postscript to the Research

1. The results of the survey suggest that the most effective sales methods are of the old-fashioned 'pressing the flesh' variety. No surprises there!
2. The survey doesn't 'say' anything about what you should do in *your* business. It just lists the preferred sales method of 247 businesses – for your business there may be a combination of techniques that you find most effective.
3. The survey doesn't show the interconnection between pre-sales and the sales process. For many, the exhibitions/events lead to the face-to-face sales meeting etc.

We knew that the survey's findings were flawed when we put together the results but we still felt that the results were of value as a starting point to get people to think hard about the return on their investment of time and money.

The Time-Money Continuum

The survey also confirmed to us that a generalisation existed:

For quick results you need to spend money on advertisements, exhibitions and mailshots.

On the other hand, if you have the time to spend and to be patient, then you can get results with little expenditure… but this method does take time.

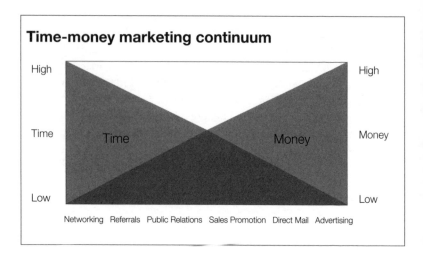

Time-money marketing continuum

The research tells us something we intuitively know – that the face-to-face and one-to-one approaches to selling are the most effective... although this might not be the case when you are selling to huge numbers of people.

THE ONE-MINUTE INTRO

Most people are dreadful at introducing their business to others because they can't explain what they do in a simple, no-nonsense way that the listener can understand. It's time to put an end to this!

Stop and Think

We are particularly bad at introducing our businesses to people or talking to people. In fact I will go further than that – most of us are ghastly at all this 'networking' stuff that so many people claim to be the new wave of the future.

The reality is that you almost certainly cannot remember the last five businesspeople you met at a party or at some event. And the reason you can't remember them is because they were not memorable. Isn't this a sad indictment on the state of affairs? People spend most of their waking hours flogging their guts out to run a better business and then you can't even remember them, never mind what their business does.

There is, however a fairly simple way to overcome this.

The Solution

Piecing together your 'One-Minute Intro' or 'Elevator Statement' is a great way to start thinking about what you are trying to do with the business.

A 'One-Minute Intro' is a succinct explanation of what you and your business do.

Give yourself a few minutes and consider the following questions. You could score yourself out of 10 where 10 is a high score and 0 is a low score.

- How well can you explain what you do to a stranger?
- Do you convince the stranger about your business?

The Point is...

Most people just open their mouths and out splutters a whole series of indecipherable jargon and gobbledegook that leaves the listener none the wiser.

Your One-Minute Intro should be easily understandable. If you are in doubt about its simplicity, try the '13 year-old test'. A 13 year-old child should easily understand your statement.

What Did You Call It?

The One-Minute Intro was originally referred to as the elevator statement; it was so called because there was a story that runs that you get into an elevator (what we call a lift in the UK) and there stands Bill Gates. He presses the button for the 10th floor and says, 'So, what do you do?'. You have 30 seconds to explain what you and your business do in a way that is convincing, compelling and memorable.

It has many other names including:
■ One-Minute Intro
■ Elevator speech
■ Audio logo
■ 30-second pitch
■ And a number of combinations of the above!

The Script

There is a formula, a script, to use to create a compelling One-Minute Intro and it goes as follows:

■ *'We work with...'*
■ *'Who have a problem with...'*
■ *'What we do is...'*
■ *'So that...'*
■ *'Which means...'*

So step-by-step, here goes...

'We Work With...'

Be specific about who you work with. You might define who you work with by one of the following:
■ Type of business
■ Age of business
■ Type of person by
   – Sex
   – Colour
   – Creed

- Religion
- Geography
- And so forth.

'Who Have A Problem With...'

Focus on what is wrong for them or what hurts. It is far more powerful. People listen up if you focus on what is wrong (their hurt) rather than focus on how nice things could be. People hear and respond to negatives better than they respond to positives.

Talk About :	Rather Than Talk About:
'...who have bad skin'	*'...who want clear skin'*
'...who miss their appointments'	*'...who want to be good time-keepers'*
'...who can't get enough customers'	*'...who want an effective marketing strategy'*
'...who can't sleep well at night'	*'...who want a good night's sleep'*

'What We Do is...'

Explain what it is that you do that resolves the problem:

- *'Test your skin type...'*
- *'Show you a structured way of managing your time...'*
- *'Provide a way of doubling your sales...'*
- *'Give you a simple device that fits on your nose...'.*

Be clear and be simple and use language that is easy to understand. This is not a sales pitch and you are not trying to prove how clever you are. All you are doing is giving them an easy-to-understand explanation of what you do.

'So That...'

Give a simple explanation of the function that the user/client/customer gets:

- *'You can use an appropriate diet and ointments...'*
- *'Log all your appointments and priorities...'*
- *'Hit your profit targets...'*
- *'You can breathe more easily...'.*

'Which Means That...'

List the benefits:

- *'You get a clean clear complexion.'*
- *'You never miss another appointment.'*
- *'You get your bonus.'*
- *'You get a great night's sleep.'*

One-minute intro

- We work with...
- Who have a problem with...
- What we do is...
- So what...
- Which means...

BENEFITS and PROOFS not FEATURES
DIFFERENCE/UNIQUENESS

And in Practice

'I work with Afro-Caribbean ladies. Who have a problem finding the right oils for their hair • What I do is import specific oils from the West Indies • So that our clients use oils that absolutely suit their hair type • Which means that they look and feel fantastic when they go on a night out.'
KM, importer of hair products and oils

'I work with the managing directors of fast-growing business • Who are feeling the pains of growth • What we do is work with them on a one-to-one basis, people who have 'been there and done it' working with people who want to go there and do it • So that you get no-nonsense solutions to your business problems from people who have had the arrows in their backs • Which means that you can exceed your targets and have the business and lifestyle that you want.'
Paul Jobin, The Directors' Centre

Checklist – One-Minute Intro

Score yourself on the scales below.

Does your One-Minute Intro:
- Sound convincing?
  No – a bit – quite a bit – yes

- Explain what your business does?
  No – a bit – quite a bit – yes

- Roll off the tongue smoothly?
  No – a bit – quite a bit – yes

- Make the listener understand what business your
  business does?
  No – a bit – quite a bit – yes

- Pass the '13 year-old test'?
  No – a bit – quite a bit – yes

*Most of us are lousy at introducing ourselves
– so here's a way of doing it properly. More
importantly, the One-Minute Intro can be used
on your website, your brochures, even your
business cards.*

ONE-MINUTE BRAND TEST

One of my favourite parts of the *Bright Marketing* workshops is what we call the 'One-Minute Brand Test'. This simple technique gets you to think about how your business is perceived by others.

'On Your Way Into Coffee...'

Going into the coffee break, delegates are instructed to take one of their business cards (or any other piece of marketing material that they might have with them, eg brochure, headed notepaper, compliments slip etc). They hand this to a conference organiser, who then staples the piece of business card/marketing material to a blank sheet of paper. All the delegates have to look at each others' marketing material and write the first thing that comes into their head on to the blank sheet of paper that accompanies the marketing material.

So, what you end up with is comments from all the other delegates on the piece of paper that has your business card/marketing material attached to it.

The comments are normally one or two words and these observations provide incredibly valuable feedback about how the viewer/recipient sees your business. The comments are honest and independent (although they may not be from your target customers).

Below is a sample of comments from a recent workshop.

And in Practice – Example One: Small Accountancy Firm

- What do all the letters stand for?
- Dull
- Boring
- Looks like a funeral directors'
- What are you trying to say?
- You obviously work from a home address
- Why have you got a hotmail address if you are a business... what does it say about you?

- A joint fax/phone number makes me think you are a one-man band
- It looks like you've printed it yourself – can't you afford a proper designer and printer or do you just not care about how professional you do (or don't) look?
- Yuck

And in Practice – Example Two: Printers

- Love the colours
- Great feel to the paper
- I can see exactly what you do
- Very bright
- Remarkable images – made me think
- Personally, I need a pair of sunglasses to look at this
- I'd get you to do my printing

So What!

Your branding can be defined as…

'the messages that leak from you like radioactivity'

So, what messages are you trying to convey and to whom?
Answer this question and you can then set about finding ways of communicating those messages.

What Messages Are You Trying To Communicate?

What are you trying to say? It could be any of the following…

- I am professional…?
- I am local…?
- I am the best in my field…?
- I am experienced…?
- I am high-tech…?
- We are a big organisation…?
- I am well-qualified…?
- We do lots of different things…?
- We only do one thing…?
- We have official approval…?
- We are modern…?

Action Point

■ The message that you are trying to communicate is:
[eg we are young-minded and modern]

....
....
....
....

■ And you are trying to communicate this to:
[eg affluent mums who want unique, high-fashion, designer outfits]

....
....
....
....

So What?

We constantly underestimate the importance of how we come across to other people. Often, we seem to measure and evaluate other people by one set of criteria and yet we don't expect them to measure and evaluate us by the same high standards that we expect of them.

All of our business communications (email, marketing materials, website, how we answer the phone, how we dress) send out messages to the outside world, whether we like it or not. To some extent we can choose which messages we wish to send out.

If we try to look at our business through the customers' eyes then we have the opportunity to select the most appropriate ways and means to communicate our intended message. Why wouldn't you want to create the best impression that would get the most positive response from your potential customer?

ASKING FOR THE BUSINESS – THREE VERSIONS

Most of us are lousy at 'asking for the business'. And if we don't ask for the business then it will go to someone else. So here are some ways to get the potential customer to buy from you.

Heard It Before?

The following quote could come from just about any boardroom of a growing business:

'We put so much of our effort into developing our product or service and then we make wonderful glossy brochures and websites that extol our virtues. We believe that our product will provide an awesome solution to the customer's problem. We even get asked to show our product to potential customers but somehow we don't always seem to get the sales that we want. So what's going on, or rather, what's going wrong?'

One-Liner

Most of us are lousy at asking for the business.

When you were a child, did you dream of becoming an award-winning master salesman? Very few of us did, yet running your own business asks you to learn those skills!

If you run your own business you must have someone in the organisation that loves selling – without sales you will go out of business. Learn how to sell. Go on a course, buy a tape, shadow a brilliant salesman…

Stop and Think

At the *Bright Marketing* seminars there is always a proportion of the audience who feel that 'in-your-face selling' is offensive and not suitable for their industry.

I agree that 'full-on' salesmen do nothing to excite me about their products; however, so many businesses seem to be too shy to 'ask for the business' – and you won't get people to buy from you unless they know that you are 'open for business! In fact the competitor that does make the effort will actually get the business.

So, if you don't want to be sales- or customer-focused then I suggest that you think about going out and getting yourself a job!

Example of Poor Salesmanship

I recently asked an on line lawyer colleague if he could give me a quote for a piece of work that I needed doing. We agreed the price and he understood that I wanted the work done as soon as possible, ideally in the next week. He didn't get back to me for 18 weeks and seemed surprised when I told him it was too late.

My point is that he just didn't seem to want the work that badly; he didn't want to work with me that much... I wasn't that important to him... and I couldn't justify spending my hard-earned money with him when there were plenty of other alternative firms who were keen (but not desperate!) to work for me!

Asking For The Business #1:
Put Your Heart On Your Sleeve

It seems to me that too many potential suppliers don't look like they want my business. They expect potential customers to pick up their enthusiasm to work together! This really isn't good enough. This is so simple but we just don't seem to 'get it'.

The power of looking people in the eye and talking directly and sincerely has a real effect. You can add to this some of the simple communication/rapport techniques that NLP (neuro-linguistic programming) and similar communication/persuasion courses suggest.

When you ask for the business, do it as if you really would like their business! Too often we expect the potential client to know, as if by osmosis, that we are really keen to work with them but we don't actually tell them so much in words!

And in Practice

'The reason I've come over to see you today is so that I can tell you how excited we are about the possibility of working with you. I just feel that we really get on well and there's a great chemistry between us; your company is just the type and size that we love to work with. So, have I made myself clear that we would relish the opportunity of working with you?'

Ian, our new health & safety consultant
When you read the words it all looks a bit cheesy but sometimes you do need to find a way of expressing your enthusiasm.

Asking For The Business #2: Get More Business Script

Here's an easy one for drumming up some more business. Again, it looks a bit over-the-top when you read the words but it does work if used appropriately.

This script is used with existing customers who already like your business. The three questions can be asked over coffee or by phone but they really do work.

'What do you love about our business?'
– just listen to what they say

'What do you hate about our business? What is it that we do that winds you up?'
– again just listen to what they say; do not try to defend anything!

'What do we need to do to get more business (or referrals?) from you?'
– and the amazing thing is that they will tell you exactly what you need to do to get more business from them!

As with all the three ways of asking for the business, you do need to have a bit of bottle to ask these questions. But if you have the courage, and most don't, then you'll watch your opportunities grow before your very eyes!

And in Practice

Jayne Seymour wrote to us that as a result of using this technique she gained seven new pieces of work (valued at over £500,000) for her communications training company. 'This was like taking candy from a baby – the work was there and I just had to ask for it... but normally I wouldn't have been so bold and so the work would probably have gone to someone else.'

Asking For The Business #3: The Referral Script

Plenty of people write at great length about referral scripts; so how do you ask for a referral?

You know that the person in front of you knows loads of people. Surely you could sell to one of them, but how do you ask for the referral so that you (and they) don't feel compromised (and you don't actually embarrass or upset the person you are talking to)?

First, those of you from professional service firms (lawyers, solicitors, accountants, architects) may feel that selling is beneath you, unprofessional and generally humiliating. Please remember that some of your competitors will not feel as precious as you and it will be them that get the business because they have had the bottle to do it when you haven't. Also, as per usual, you will not die!

Part of the trick is to get the respondent to give the answer 'yes' to every one of your questions. This makes it easier for them to agree to help (there's a bit of psychology going on here!). You will need to adapt the script to your business but most successful scripts go roughly as follows...

'As you know we are trying to grow our business.'
'Yes.'

'You were happy with our product/service when we last provided it to you.'
'Yes.'

'You must know lots of people in your industry who could also benefit from our product/service.'
'Yes.'

'It would be rude of me to ask you for their names and then phone them up because that would be like a cold call and that would hack-off everyone.'
'Yes.'

'Well… this is what I'd like you to do. Call these people and tell them about what I did for you and tell them that I will call. This way everyone wins… you win because you get brownie points from your colleague, because in the interests of goodwill (and good networking) you will have recommended someone that you trust… your colleagues win because they get the name of a reliable, tried and trusted, supplier. I win because I get the opportunity to show my product to a good lead. Everyone wins. So, are you happy to make those calls? Is that OK?'
'Yes.'

Let me just run through this again, line by line, to explain exactly what is going on…

'As You Know We Are Trying To Grow Our Business.'
This is a better way of asking for business than saying, 'We are hungry and haven't had a new customer for ages…'

'You Were Happy With Our Product/Service When We Last Provided It To You.'
You will only be running through this process with someone who is a fan of your business. And as long as you have been doing some form of customer satisfaction questionnaires then you will know what people think about your service. The sad thing is that so many businesses don't actually know what your customers really think as they don't ask often enough… do you know what every one or even some of your customers actually think of you?

'You Must Know Lots Of People In Your Industry Who Could Also Benefit From Our Product/Service.'
This is what you are trying to get to… you are asking them to (subconsciously) turn on their brain and think about who they know that could benefit from your product. They are also getting ready for some kind of 'hit' because this is following a fairly standard scripted sales pitch… so you need to retain their confidence and make sure that their credibility and reputation will not be tarnished or compromised, so the next thing you say is…

'It Would Be Rude Of Me To Ask You For Their Names And Then Phone Them Up Because That Would Be Like A Cold Call And That Would Hack-Off Everyone.'

This wins back their confidence in you because you're starting to take away their fear.

'Well… This Is What I'd Like You To Do. Call These People And Tell Them About What I Did For You And Tell Them That I Will Call. This Way Everyone Wins… You Win Because You Get Brownie Points From Your Colleague, Because In The Interests Of Goodwill (And Good Networking) You Will Have Recommended Someone That You Trust… Your Colleagues Win Because They Get The Name Of A Reliable, Tried And Trusted, Supplier. I Win Because I Get The Opportunity To Show My Product To A Good Lead. Everyone Wins. So, Are You Happy To Make Those Calls? Is That OK?'

The funny thing is that in nine out of 10 cases the client says 'Yes, of course' and if you're in their office when you have the conversation then they actually make the calls in front of you!

And in Practice

'I hate to admit it, especially as I am marketing director of a plc, but I had forgotten all about asking for referrals. We'd been trying to get into two particular multinationals for ages and, as a last resort, (and after hearing you speak!) I went for the referrals route. I used your referral script and specifically named the people I was trying to reach and within five calls I had not one but two introductions to the target we had been trying to get in front of. The two deals, which are going ahead, are worth more than several million pounds to us!'

A friend, JP, who wishes to remain anonymous!

Your whole business depends on getting sales; selling is probably the key skill you cannot afford to skimp on. Someone, somewhere in your business must be able to ask for the business and do it so that they win the sales. Every degree of mediocrity in your sales skills will directly reduce the profitability and success of your business. Ask for the business, now!

THE 80:20 RULE – THE LAW OF THE VITAL FEW FOR YOUR BUSINESS

The 80:20 Rule is such a key concept in this book that you will have noticed it mentioned more than several times, for instance, in the discussions where the best sales methods were considered (see page 41).

Question

What would happen if you sacked 50% of your least profitable customers and worked more with the rest, the profitable ones?!

The 80:20 Principle, also known as Pareto's Principle, is a classic of management science. In fact it is such a classic that most people have forgotten all about it or they have forgotten how it applies in so many instances.

Writing in the late 19th Century, Pareto noticed that with an amazing regularity, things were not distributed evenly. A few people earned the majority of the money, a few people possessed most of the wealth, and a few animals were larger than the rest. This has been translated into the 80:20 Rule.

So What?

The implications of the Pareto Principle are several for your business. The upside of the principle is that some of your inputs are incredibly effective.

eg 20% of customers generate 80% of your profit.

On the other hand, Pareto also implies incredible inefficiencies.

eg the other 20% of your profit (a fraction really) is delivered by 80% of your customers (the majority).

Using the 80:20Rule to your advantage then you can do the following:

■ Focus on what works

> **Fact**
>
> 20% of inputs cause 80% of outputs.
>
> The 80:20 Rule in business says that 20% of salesmen get 80% of your sales. 20% of your customers deliver 80% of your profit. 20% of your time creates 80% of your outputs. This is the Law of the Vital Few and the Trivial Many.

- Recognise that you become progressively less effective/ profitable
- Concentrate on the vital few and try to cut the trivial many – focus on becoming more effective – otherwise you will become the proverbial busy fool.
- Don't chase the perfect solution – the more time you spend on a problem, the less value you add – so it is better to do the big stuff, the powerful thinking and get the right basic shape to a solution rather than always concentrate on the detail, the minutiae.

Action Point

Is it true that the majority of profit comes from a small minority of your clients or client types?
Yes/No

Is it true that many of your clients are not making you any money at all?
Yes/No

Is it true that some of your clients are losing you money?
Yes/No

So, what are you going to do about it?

....

....

....

....

....

....

....

....

....

....

....

Action Point

Instructions

■ Write down a list of your 'Top 10' clients by profitability –
what do they have in common?
[eg Company A, B, C... they are all buying more than
£100,000 pa]

....
....
....
....
....
....
....
....
....
....

■ More importantly, where can you find more like them?
[eg they are all big players in the key trade organisation]

....
....
....
....
....

■ Write down a list of your 'Bottom 10' clients – what do
they have in common?
[eg Company X, Y, Z... they are all buying less than
£50,000 pa and most are only interested in the products
that are tricky to deliver]

....
....
....
....
....
....
....
....
....

■ What are you going to do with these businesses?
[eg put prices up by 20% on orders for the tricky
products and/or orders less than £50,000 to make sure
that it is worth our while if we are going to work on these
kinds of contracts]

....

....

....

....

The 80/20 Principle

20% of customers generate 80% of profit!

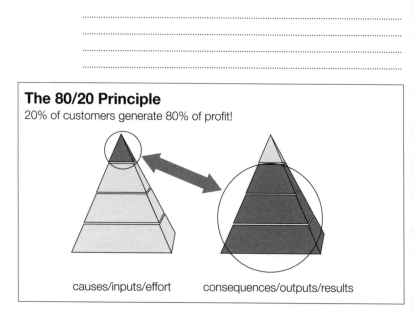

causes/inputs/effort   consequences/outputs/results

Why Should I Care?

Sensible application of the 80:20 Rule leads to massive
improvements in effectiveness. The maths works and
applying the 80:20 for the first time normally evokes a real
'Aha!' moment as you realise how you can become so much
more effective by concentrating on what really works.

And in Practice

Leo Gibson (name changed) ran a chain of guitar shops in the north
and north-east, with a steadily declining turnover and even faster
declining profitability. He was incensed when shown the 80:20 Principle
and launched a full frontal attack which went something like...
'You don't understand my kind of business... hundreds of irritating
kids swamp us and want to try our budget $99 Fenders (made in

the Far East with no profit margins left for us) and after visiting the shop 10 times they then buy the things online from someone else who can sell them at pretty much the price that we get them for – we can't compete – and these kids are a pain in the backside: rude, noisy, and a total waste of time… and then people like you swan in and go for the top range $3,000 guitars, the ones with the big profit margins! We're in big trouble and your theory doesn't help! Obviously I've got to find a way of selling my guitars to these kids even though there's no money in it.'

Of course, the answer was in the 80/20 Principle. Like most businesses, he did get 80% of profit from 20% of customers… and over half of his customers at the bottom end made him virtually no money at all. So I asked, 'What would happen if you sacked 50% of your customers and focused on getting more of the rich ones, getting a bigger share of their wallet?'. The question stopped Leo in his tracks.

Four Months Later

I met up with Leo again after four months – he had bitten the bullet and gone out of his way to encourage the premium customers to buy the $1000+ guitars and discouraged the cheap and cheerful range customers by various methods. The result: turnover up 60% on the previous year!; profits up 100% on the previous year. By discouraging the unprofitable kids, the pond life, he made the more sophisticated (and more profitable) customers more comfortable and less distracted and more willing to part with their money. So, although the number of sales reduced, the value and profitability of each sale increased dramatically.

Here's a radical suggestion… what would happen if you sacked the bottom 50% of your customers, the ones with no real prospects that consume most of your time and effort and probably cost you more than they earn you?

PUT UP PRICES

People always ask about whether to put up prices or reduce them. Please, please, think very carefully before you consider putting prices down. Let me explain my thinking.

The Road To Bankruptcy

The road to bankruptcy is paved with people who tried to buy market share by cutting prices. Always try to avoid a price war, as it is unlikely that you will be the winner. There is always a bigger player who has bigger marketing power, bigger buying power and deeper pockets. You will end up reducing your margins... some competitors/people may go out of business... (they euphemistically describe this as a 'shakeout' in the industry!). And you'll get less profit per sale than you got before. To me this is like trying to run up the down escalator!

The other option is to raise prices.

What Happens When You Raise Prices?

Inevitably you will lose some customers when you put up prices. However, the clients you normally lose are those that are 'buying on price' – to me these are normally what I would describe as 'pond life', clients you would be happy to see the back of... those that bought on price, often paid late and always want more. You don't need these types of clients.

And the irony is... that your most profitable clients often don't notice the change in prices because they aren't buying on price alone; they are buying on quality or value-added.

Price Changes In A Nutshell

To summarise, lowering prices probably attracts the wrong clients and eats into your profitability. Raising prices means you lose the pond life and become more profitable. I know which one I prefer.

Below are two tables. You can use the tables to calculate how much your sales volume must change to compensate for a change in price (and still keep the same gross profit margin).

Table To Calculate Percentage Sales Volume Decrease As A Result Of Price Increases At Various Gross Margin % Levels To Maintain Same Gross Margin

% price increase ▼	Existing percentage gross margin								
	5	10	15	20	25	30	35	40	50
	Percentage unit/volume decrease to generate same gross margin								
2.0	29	17	12	9	7	6	5	5	4
3.0	37	23	17	13	11	9	8	7	6
4.0	44	29	21	17	14	12	10	9	7
5.0	50	33	25	20	17	14	12	11	9
7.5	60	43	33	27	23	20	18	16	13
10.0	67	50	40	33	29	25	22	20	17
15.0	75	60	50	43	37	33	30	27	23

Table To Calculate Percentage Sales Volume Increase As A Result Of Price Reductions At Various Gross Margin % Levels To Maintain Same Gross Margin

% price increase ▼	Existing percentage gross margin								
	5	10	15	20	25	30	35	40	50
	Percentage unit/volume decrease to generate same gross margin								
2.0	67	25	15	11	9	7	6	5	4
3.0	150	43	25	18	14	11	9	8	6
4.0	400	67	36	25	19	15	13	11	9
5.0		100	50	33	25	20	17	14	11
7.5		300	100	60	43	33	27	23	18
10.0			200	100	67	50	40	33	25
15.0				300	150	100	75	60	43

An Example

- You sell units at £10.00   £10.00
- You buy them at £7.00   £7.00
- So, your gross margin is 30% (3/10 x100)   £3.00

Using the first chart, to calculate the impact of an *increase* in price of say 10%…

With a GP of 30%, the impact of increasing price by 10% (from £10.00 to £11.00) would be that you could afford to lose 25% of sales volume before you would lose any gross profit.

Using the second chart, to calculate the impact of a decrease in price of say 10%...

With a GP of 30%, the impact of decreasing price by 10% (from £10.00 to £9.00) would be that you would have to increase your sales volume by at least 50% before you would simply match your earlier gross profit.

If you put prices down by 10% you would need to sell 50% more units to stay in the same place in terms of cash in you back pocket... So if you were working Monday to Friday, then, all things being equal you would now need to work another two and a half days a week... in other words, Saturday, Sunday and next Monday morning!

If you put your prices up by 10% then you could afford to lose 25% of your sales turnover. You lose the price-sensitive clients and you could have a day off!

I know which one I would prefer.

And in Practice

RHT, the outside catering company that specialise in pop festivals, were turning over $950,000 with a gross margin of 40% (after all direct costs). Judi, the owner, was considering the impact of price changes.

The tables clearly indicated the following:
- A price increase of 4% would mean that she would generate the same gross margin ($s) even if sales volumes fell by 9%
- A price increase of 5% would mean that she would generate the same gross margin ($s) even if sales volumes fell by 11%
- A price increase of 10% would mean that she would generate the same gross margin ($s) even if sales volumes fell by 20%.

Judi:
'I decided to put prices up by 10% on the assumption that trade may slow down a little, but the benefits would go straight down to the bottom line – I reckon that most punters are not too price sensitive, within reason, and we are currently seen to be on the cheap side.'

'The gamble paid off. Volumes did drop but only by a small amount, later calculated to be about 5%. The net effect was beneficial to all – less activity, less output, greater profits.'

Judi's story tells us to be brave with our pricing. It is rarely clever to lower your prices because of the damage to your bottom line – you end up being busier and with less profit per transaction.

Action Point: Focus On The Profitable Lines And Drop The Under-Performers

■ Where do you make the real profit in the business?
  [eg specific clients or products or geographical areas...]

....

....

....

....

■ What products/lines generate the real profit?
  [eg specific clients or products or geographical areas...]

....

....

....

....

■ And what activities generate no profit?
  [eg specific clients or products or geographical areas...]

....

....

....

....

Once you have asked yourself these questions you should be able to focus on doing more with the highly profitable. At the same time you must deal with the under-performers – drop the under-performing products and services; drop the unprofitable customers. Don't accept the excuses such as 'non-profitable work is required to cover overhead' or other such nonsense.

It's the 80:20 Rule again! When looking at the profitables, look for the 80/20 Principle – 80% of outputs (profit) will be generated by 20% of inputs (customers/products/effort). The 'bright marketer' sees the 80:20 in nearly everything they do! You should always be looking for ways to be more effective while looking for ways to cut out the ineffective!

THE EXPERT

All roads seem to lead to the notion that the well-managed expert's business can win the business...

- **People like to buy from an expert and not from a follower**
- **One accountant is better than another because the client thinks that he/she is...; marketing is not a battle for the product but for the mind of the customer**

Here are some more examples of how and why most roads do seem to lead to this idea that it is the 'expert business' not just the expert that wins:

- Most PSFs (Professional Service Firms or experts) think that their knowledge and operations performance is more important than skill/attitude – they are wrong!
- You probably know more than most in your chosen field if you read the key two texts in the field AND understand them – most people don't!
- Most experts are technicians and don't understand what people really *buy*
- Most experts are technicians and don't understand what people really *need* from them
- Most experts are technicians and don't understand what people really *want* from them
- Most experts are technicians and don't understand the importance of good bedside manner
- Most experts are technicians and were trained to be technically excellent but no-one told them how to run a service-based business
- Most experts are technicians and don't understand the importance of demonstrating benefits/proofs/ testimonials
- Most experts are technicians and don't understand the business development process.

You should become an expert – become an expert in the world that you work in.

People hate buying from a 'follower' or an 'also-ran' but love buying from an expert… whether you are an accountant, a homeopath or a plumber, you can become the expert business in your market.

And because everyone will know and see you as the expert… they will ask you to do the work and they will pay a premium price!

What Does An Expert Do?

1. **An Expert Focuses** – they have a focus on specific people (target customers) who have specific problems and issues. Experts have their own One–Minute Intro sorted and defined, focusing on target clients and benefits.
2. **An Expert Writes** – how tos, white papers, research, surveys, articles, columns, books(?), '10 Things To Know About…', 'Impact Of New Legislation…'.
3. **An Expert Possesses** – a website, knowledge, a Filofax to die for…
4. **An Expert Knows** – the movers and shakers, influencers, key people in their world or at least they have access to them.
5. **An Expert Speaks** – at the Chamber, networking events, workshops, seminars, business clubs, masterclasses and so on…

As well as the five attributes above there are two additional, yet underpinning, concepts:

6. **An Expert Has An 'Ology'** and a system.
7. **An Expert Uses The Power Of Testimonials, Endorsements and Stories.**

Once you clarify your specialisation then you can walk and talk and write about it (using the same case studies or examples) to confirm your expert status. Each element of *The Expert!* model supports the others.

Experts present themselves in the position of authority or knowledge; they tend to be seen as what some might call 'positioners'; they present themselves as 'positioners' (where they set out to adopt a specific position in the eyes of the customer) rather than 'prospectors' (where 'prospectors' are chasing work and clients).

The purpose of most expert activity is to command respect rather than to hustle for business. Often, experts take on what can be described as an 'education-based' marketing approach to attracting new clients; and this education includes giving away valuable information and advice rather than giving a sales pitch.

The mindset of the successful expert is that:

- Their activity gets them the prospects that they want
- They maintain their dignity and professionalism because they are not using heavy-handed sales techniques... they let interested parties come to them – a client pull/ attraction approach
- They are educating and showing people how their expertise can help
- They establish credibility and this recognition is a key driver in personal satisfaction
- They have a systematic process for communicating and for delivering work, which means that they are not constantly re-inventing the wheel.

Stop and Think

A simple question from me to you...

'So, what's holding you back?'

Why Do We Need The Expert! Model?

Put simply, most professional service firms make life very difficult for themselves.

The really small ones have no idea how to run a business; they spend most of their time struggling to find clients; the larger ones may be more successful but also struggle to keep clients in an ever-changing world where the clients, competitors and staff seem to be constantly changing their behaviour.

Question

When most firms in your industry look pretty similar (actually almost identical) then why should people bother to buy from you when they can buy from the competition?

The Expert!

Speaks...
- Forums, conferences, exhibitions
- Seminars, workshops, masterclasses

Focuses...
- One-Minute Intro
- Work with...
- Feel... Problem with...
- What we do is...
- Which means...
- So what....

Writes...
- Pamphlets, booklets, how tos
- Newsletters
- White papers
- Articles: local, trade, national
- Books, ebooks

Knows...
- Movers & shakers
- Connected
- Influencer
- Known

Possesses...
- Website
- Discussion forum
- Database
- Knowledge

+ an 'ology'/system
+ testimonials

Steps to Becoming an Expert

1. Assess/outline your current expertise
2. Find your first draft Focus and One-Minute Intro
3. Agree your first draft Focus and One-Minute Intro
4. Audit – who is the competition and what is their Point of View (PoV)
5. Build on own Gaps/Strengths
6. Create own Point of View
7. Collect Evidence to support your Point of View
8. Identify Patterns
9. Create, Explain and Articulate a Proprietary Point of View
10. Create your system – the way that you do things
11. Create and Refine Final One-Minute Intro – use it for networking, your biog, brochures, your website, marketing literature...
12. Create White Paper
13. Create Marketing Kit (see Marketing Pack chapter)
14. Write Articles, How Tos, White Papers
15. Photoshoot, if appropriate
16. Biog/brochure/website as appropriate (using One-Minute Intro)
17. CD-Rom/Showreel/brochure or whatever is appropriate (using One-Minute Intro)
18. Testimonials – gather them
19. Sort the Brand, Website...

20. Look for opportunities to:
    - ■ Speak
    - ■ Get in print
    - ■ Network
    - ■ Publish.

And in Practice

Fred Edwards, MD of myFD (www.myfd.com) took the Expert model to heart, 'We saw the logic of the Expert model and started to apply it to our business. We provide a new sort of service that delivers finance directors and finance controller skill in a relatively crowded market space. To non-finance people interims and part-timers look similar; all our competitors look similar; after all we are all FDs with FD training and FD backgrounds. What we did was apply the Expert model: we focused on our target customers' hurts and how we could solve the pains for them, we started writing articles and getting our PR machine working,
we tidied up the website and got networking both in person and online and started to be asked to speak about what we had written about.

'Very quickly we got known by the people who we wanted to know about us – we stood out from our competitors because we were the only ones speaking at seminars and we were being talked about and being quoted in the right places – we focused on running and growing a business (working 'on' the business as well as working 'in' it). The whole thing is a benevolent cycle and pretty quickly we saw our sales funnel fill like never before. Such a simple set of techniques that have
a real power when combined.'

If only most experts would realise the difference between being an expert (technically) and running an expert business (an expert who is in business!).

PUT IT ALL TOGETHER – THE 'CUSTOMER IS KING' SEVEN-POINT PLAN

My earlier book, 'Customer Is King' showed a step-by-step process for getting your business to see itself through your customers' eyes. This approach will make sure that you design a business that delivers on its promise and delights its customers.

The seven points of the customer experience plan are as follows:

1. Redefine your business as a problem-solver
2. Understand the real scope of your business
3. Get under each customer's skin!
4. Stand out to be outstanding
5. Develop a strategy to define your position
6. Calculate just how much a customer is worth to you
7. Select your weapons

The seven-point plan is all about great questions. For instance:

- Who are your customers? What do they want?
- What is the 'promise'? How well do you deliver the 'promise'?
- What do your customers think of you?
- What people do you want to be your customers? What do you want them to think of you?
- What are you selling? What are they buying?
- Really what are they buying? Really what are you selling?
- What could you do right now to improve your sales?
- How can you improve your skills?
- How can you get better customers? What do you mean by better customers?

Can you add your own questions to this list?

#1 Redefine Your Business As A Problem-solver

To get to the heart of what your business does, you need to redefine yourself. Is this the stuff that marketing books should be about? I think so. Becoming a problem-solver allows you to help your clients in a very different way from 'business as usual'.

What Problem are You Solving? What's the Real Problem?

Sometimes you need to change how you see yourself – change the perception that you are using to look at the world. To understand the customer experience and to take advantage of it, redefine yourself as a problem-solver!

If you put yourself in the role of 'problem-solver' for your clients, you start to look for problems to solve. Rather than looking for sales, you look for the problems that the client is facing. By focusing on the customers' problems a number of things happen:

- You start to see things through the customer's eyes
- You start to see real issues that the customer faces
- You are able to have more empathy as you try to see what help the client might need
- You develop a stronger relationship because you are not constantly wearing your 'sales hat'
- You are developing long-term rather than short-term relationships.

By running your business as if it is a problem-solver, suddenly you have a significant role to play for the customer. Your role is that of figuring out what your customers are trying to do and helping them to do it. Wearing this different pair of spectacles, the world takes on a different shape.

Action Point

Answer the following for your business:

First the typical *BM*-type 'why' questions.

■ Why do people come to your business?

....
....
....

■ Why do people buy your product/service?

....
....
....

■ Why do they buy it from you?

....
....
....

Some typical 'what' questions

■ What problems do they have that you are trying to solve?

....
....
....

■ What would their ideal solution be? (What should they
  be saying, thinking and doing as a result of visiting your
  business)

....
....
....

■ What is your ideal solution? (What should they be saying,
  thinking and doing as a result of visiting your business)

....
....
....

Now, for a moment, forget about the need to make a sale.
Ask:

■ If you use the mindset of a problem-solver, what
else could you be doing to make life easier for your
customer? [eg telling them about their competitors,
tell them about potential customers/suppliers,
recommend some new software/supplier you've just
got, give honest feedback on their poor website/
adverts/salesmen/receptionist etc]

....
....
....

And in Practice

The feedback was: *'Did you know that your clever clogs software falls over
on my machine and I am not the only person who has this problem?'*. It was
only when the feedback was personal, director to director, that the
lady concerned realised that she had some serious issues (her sales
and her technical staff had been somewhat economic with the truth,
hiding behind a mantra that the customers were stupid). As a result,
a new technical team was put in place with the skills to sort and de-
bug the software. In hindsight, the business would not have survived
another six months of trading. Someone has to tell a director how
things really are because the truth is often so difficult to establish.
The result for the carrier of the bad news: a loyal and very grateful
customer for life!

Clearly it can be a high-risk strategy to give feedback when it is
not asked for, especially if the feedback is, shall we say, rather
bold. However, you will be remembered for this and as long as
you couch your feedback in the spirit of help and assistance then
you should be thanked and remembered for it. I love it when
people (suppliers and clients) send us emails saying *'Did you know
that your...'* Obviously we didn't know or obviously we would have
done something about it and it's great to know that someone cares
enough to take the trouble to help us. I love it.

#2 Understand The Real Scope Of Your Business

Most of us regularly undersell ourselves. As well as underselling ourselves, we regularly misunderstand how we are perceived; there is often a gap between what we think we do and what the customer sees.

In a personality, a gap between your own self-image (of how you present yourself to others), and how others perceive you, can result in serious mental disorders. These may result in you getting locked up! In a business, such a gap results in dissatisfied customers and poor performance.

So

■ Do you ever get carried away with the features of your product and forget that the customer may not be on the same wavelength as you?
Yes/No

■ Do you ask enough questions of your customers?
Yes/No

■ Do you really listen to your customers and what they want?
Yes/No

If you have too narrow a vision of what you offer to customers then you will undersell yourself, you will miss opportunities to develop the relationship. If, on the other hand you understand the scope and depth of how you can help, then you will discover new opportunities to work with and help your customer.

Expand the limits of how you define your business. Consider how you could expand into new or different products/ service lines and/or new or different markets. Think laterally. Consider the advantages and disadvantages of becoming broader in your scope or becoming narrower/deeper in your scope.

#3 Get Under Each Customer's Skin!

Getting under the skin of your customer is no easy task. Nearly every business is trying to find out what makes their customers tick. Endless customer surveys by market research companies try to figure out how to sell more products to the poor unsuspecting(?) customers.

Keep Asking the Tough *BM*-type Questions

- Who's the product for?
- What or who is your target market?
- Why do people buy the product? Why do they buy from you?
- What does it feel like to be one of your customers?
- Do you delight your customers?
- What would you have to do to be known for 'legendary customer service'? What would the effect be?
- What would happen if you sacked your bottom 50% of customers right now?
- Could you work out 20 ways to get closer to the other 50% of your customers? Could you get a bigger share of their wallets?
- Can you identify or create the 'ambassadors' (the raving fans!) for your business?

To get under the customers' skin there are various options for the research – some traditional, some more innovative:

- Customer Focus Groups
- Run a survey on the net via a discussion forum
- Use a student – get a student to do a so-called university research project
- Run a private dinner/event for opinion formers
- While writing an article for a trade paper you can interview your customers and feature their comments in the article
- Run a conference or a seminar
- Run a special Suppliers' Seminar
- Run a Customers' Day

Why Should You Be Doing This?

Somehow you've got to find ways of being more than just in tune with your customers. To get ahead of your competitors you need to understand what it is that your customers want and to demonstrate that you must understand what they want and need, and be able to do it better than your competitors.

Action Point

Jot down the names of your 10 best customers. Next, contact each one, and ask:

- What do you really like about the way we do business?
- What drives you mad about the way we do business?
- If you ran my business what five changes would you make and why?
- What opportunities am I missing?
- If we are going to grow the business, what aspects must we keep and what must we lose?
- What could we do that would make you want to buy more from us?
- What do you think our other customers think about us?
- Who do you see as our main competitors and how are they better or worse than us?

This exercise will give you plenty to think about.

The Point is...

There should be a whole book on getting under the customers' skin. The point is that the more that you understand and empathise with the needs, concerns and worries of each customer then the greater your chances of offering a product or service that matches or exceeds their aspirations. As a side-effect, you will increase the chances of making more sales by showing your interest and curiosity and by establishing your credentials as 'more than just a supplier' by proving that you are a real human being. This process will put you ahead of the competition!

#4 To Stand Out Is To Be Outstanding

If you are the same as the rest then why should customers bother to buy from you? You ignore the one-liner at your peril! Wake up and smell the coffee! In a world where competition seems to be everywhere, you need to separate yourself from the rest.

If you compete on price, only the customer will win – the company with the lowest prices (ie biggest buying power) will get the business. This is no place for the timid.

Key Point

People prefer the brand that they think/believe will give them what they want; marketing is usually a battle of perceptions more than a battle of products. In today's world you have to try much harder to create (and maintain) the perceived difference.

If you want to be more successful at creating and maintaining the perceived difference of your product, then the customers' experience should be made to be unique in tangible, physical ways. A corollary to this is that if your service is intangible then a powerful way of branding yourself is by creating tangible (and ideally memorable) experiences.

Same/Better/Wow!?

The Same/Better/Wow! Index is a great tool for looking at an existing product or service or for looking at a new one. It is not for the light-hearted because it's whole purpose is to get you to design and deliver something extraordinary – so if

Fact

Brand preference has always been a function of perception.

you are happy with mediocrity then this tool is not for you! And if you are in a situation where you are not prepared to really improve what you offer your customers then again, this is not for you.

So, what is this index? It is a simple yet profound tool that can be used in workshops to look at your own product or that of your competitors.

First, you breakdown your offering into its component parts, the 'customer touch points' (how and when and where we affect the customer's experience) of becoming a customer. You then score each part:

- ■ 'Same' – no better – probably about the same – as the competition
- ■ 'Better' – something that is probably a little better than that provided by your competitors
- ■ 'Wow' – really amazing in some sense; it takes your breath away.

Why Should I Care About Customer Touch Points?

If you can see what it feels like to be a customer experiencing your service then you can set about improving it. Identifying and recognising each step of the journey allows you to improve those steps that are not satisfactory.

And in Practice

Designing a new, so-called better programme, Jim McPherson realised that all training programmes do look about the same. Jim set out to design a new programme. First he outlined his design and started to draft out the marketing materials and so forth. Next, he used the Same/Better/Wow! Index to calibrate the offering that he was designing. His scoresheet looked as follows:

The Same/Better/Wow! Index – My product v. The Competition

Component:	Same	Better	Wow!
Marketing Materials		☺	
Quality of Telesales	☺		
Quality of Email Communication	☺		
Joining Instructions	☺		
Pre-Course Worksheet		☺	
Administration	☺		
Welcome at the Venue	☺		
Signposting at the Venue	☺		
Venue Hospitality	☺		
Speaker Presentations		☺	
Speaker-Audience Contact		☺	

Ideas/Concepts/Course Content   ☺
Handout Materials   ☺
Visuals   ☺
Post-Course Follow-up   ☺
Changes in Delegate Behaviour   ☺
Changes in Delegate's Business Performance   ☺

This index spurred him on to figure out what he would have to do to get at least a third of the scores in the 'Wow!' column and less than a third in the 'same' column.

Jim now runs a powerhouse training company, a number one in its field.

Component:	Same	Better	Wow!
Marketing Materials			
Quality of Telesales			
Quality of Email Communication			
Joining Instructions			
Pre-Course Worksheet			
Administration			
Welcome at the Venue			
Signposting at the Venue			
Venue Hospitality			
Speaker Presentations			
Speaker-Audience Contact			
Ideas/Concepts/Course Content			
Handout Materials			
Visuals			
Post-Course Follow-up			
Changes in Delegate Behaviour			
Changes in Delegate's Business Performance			

Action Point

Consider your worst performing product or service. Using the index template below, decide the key components, and then score each of them. How do you perform? Taking each component, think of three things that you could do to improve the performance. Even better, do this exercise with a customer!

When you take your best product or service and map out its Same/Better/Wow! scores, what are the areas that you are consistently scoring well in? What themes are emerging about what you are good at or where you delight customers? Always look at such an exercise through the customers' eyes. What learning points do you take away from this? And, what are you going to do as a result?

#5 Develop A Strategy To Define Your Position

A cool and calm analysis of your business environment will consider key factors that may influence how you should consider and plan your future.

Key strategy questions include:
- How good are you?
- Who are your customers today/tomorrow?
- Who are your competitors today/tomorrow?
- What is going on in the market today/tomorrow?
- What is going on in the industry today/tomorrow?
- What is going on in the world today/tomorrow?

(See also the chapters on strategy in *Kick-Start Your Business*)

Positioning is at the heart of strategy formulation for your business. It is one of the hardest parts of the 're-inventing your business' scenario that is being considered. For some business people, it is relatively easy to understand what positioning is and how to do it. The difficulty comes in the execution, the doing bit.

Positioning is all about understanding 'the map' of where (and how and against whom) you are competing. Positioning is a difficult process. Positioning is a creative, subjective process. Positioning helps you understand why you are different

or points to how you could emphasise your difference.
Positioning suggests a version of the territory; it is a map.

Doing 'Positioning' In Three Steps

How do you differ from your competitors? As a consequence
of understanding how you differ, you can then focus
your actions and your communications on what makes
you different. Remember that if you are the same as your
competition, then why should clients bother to buy from you?

Establishing the business' position is a three-part process.

STEP ONE: List your competitors and list which customers or customer segments each competitor is aimed at

Draw up a list of your key competitors. Next to each
competitor, list the customers or target customer segments
that the competitor focuses on. What will emerge is that
different competitors are focusing on different niches or
sub-sectors of the market.

STEP TWO: Write down your niche

In other words, which customers or customer segment are
you aimed at?

Be specific about whom you aim your business activities at.
Consider your key competitors for those customers.

Often we work so hard to get the product out of the
factory gate that we forget to remind ourselves exactly what
we are trying to do. More importantly, we need to have a
thorough understanding of the competitive environment
that we are competing in.

STEP THREE: Establish your position

Establishing your position is a very ambiguous process –
be warned. It helps you to understand your competitive
environment. Just because it is ambiguous doesn't mean
that you shouldn't do it.

The position is mapped out in what is called a brand-
positioning matrix. Essentially, it is a box. The box has two
different axes that allow you to map out the competing
businesses according to how they score on the respective axes.

At its simplest level, you decide the titles of the axes. The purpose is to find axes that emphasise the difference between you and your competitors (in the eyes of the customer).

What to put on the axes? It is time for a bit of creativity here. Look at your business through your customers' eyes. If you interviewed a customer, what might be the criteria that they would use to measure you, as compared with others in your industry? Eg Smarter? Faster? Higher tech? More rigorous? Cheaper? Cleaner? Friendlier?

Take several of the criteria that might be applied to your business and see which ones create some kind of a space between you and the competition.

Eg if the criterion is fast, does this suggest that most of your competitors are much slower? If the criterion is younger, does this suggest that your competition is mostly much older?

Eventually you will have two criteria for the two axes. You might have: bespoke – standard solution; local – national; traditional – hyper-modern; high-tech – low-tech; metropolitan – provincial; indoors – outdoors; cheap – expensive; people-led – market-led and so on. You need to go through the motions of doing this exercise on paper. Reading about it will not make you get a better understanding of your business. Finding the right combination of axes is the tough part. If you are able to separate yourself 'from the rest' then this becomes the difference that you can focus on.

The case study below will explain how the matrix works in action.

And in Practice

Jim McPherson's training business, struggled to establish some kind of 'uniqueness' in its early days. After using the Same/Better/Wow! Index, Jim worked on positioning – this method would help him to see the differences between him and his competitors in terms of the overall offering to customers.

After several hours of trying out different combinations of headings for the axes, Jim's management team finally found a set of headings that would separate themselves out from the rest. The headings chosen were:

- Type of output/work done
- Style of dealing with clients

Competitors:
- Big Training Companies
- Business Schools
- Government/Business Support Agencies
- Independent Freelance Trainers

Axis 1: type of output: A scale between boutique and generalist emerged	
Big Training Companies	Very generalist on the whole – claim to be experts in most fields
Business Schools	Very generalist on the whole – claim to be experts in most fields
Government/Business Support Agencies	Very generalist on the whole – claim to be experts in most fields
Independents	Very specialist, usually
Jim's Training Business	Very specialist

Axis 2: style:	
A scale between theoretical/research/agenda-based training and highly practical/challenging emerged	
Big Training Companies	Driven by the teaching agenda
Business Schools	Driven by the teaching agenda
Government/Business Support Agencies	Usually driven by the teaching agenda
Independents	Driven by teaching agenda as well as listening to client needs
Jim's Training Business	Obsessed by the clients – very practical – needs

If you plot the two axes onto a matrix and plot the various positions of the differing competitors your map looks as below.

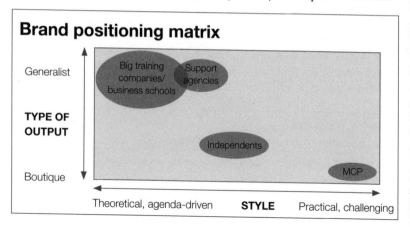

What you can see from the positioning matrix is that your selection of axes has enabled us to define a unique positioning. This can be used to emphasise the difference between the business and its competitors.

For instance, your advertising copy or sales pitch could run along the lines of:

'Whereas most training companies are focused on their own teaching agenda, we are quite the opposite. We focus on client needs.' Or, 'If you want a generalist training company go to the others. But if you want a training company who is more interested in a deep understanding of the subject of leadership, then come to us!'

The Point is...

The positioning exercise enables you to define your own niche. And the purpose of developing your niche is to make your business different, or even unique, in its category.

#6 Calculate Just How Much A Customer Is Worth To You

Do you know how much a customer is worth to you? Unless you know the true value of a customer (to your business) then how can you decide how much you are prepared to spend to acquire one?

Customers are often worth more to us than we realise. This is particularly true in the case of services. You need to know how much it costs to acquire a client and how much the typical client is worth to you. Only then can you decide how much you are prepared to spend to acquire a new client!

Definition

'Relationship marketing' is about maximising long-term profitability through the intelligent use of information. The information is used to enhance and to create superior relationships with customers.

Customer Lifetime Value

Customer lifetime value is at the heart of relationship marketing. Data-warehousing and data-mining are the tools used in bigger businesses.

In traditional marketing each client is valued on a year-by-year basis, focusing on profit per annum. This approach created a gap between the measurement system and the real world. In the real world it may take some time to make a customer profitable. Remember, customers do not stop and start with the financial year. It may take several years for your investment in a relationship to pay-off.

Customer lifetime value is a way of considering the value of a customer across their anticipated life with the company. It acknowledges that the investment a company makes in acquiring a new customer may not be repaid with the first purchase or even the first year of purchases!

#7 Select Your Weapons

You can only think about how to spend your marketing budget after you know who you are trying to reach and what you are trying to say to them.

My view is simple.

Unless you know what you are trying to communicate, and to whom and why, then you cannot effectively choose the most appropriate tools. Only think about which tools (or weapons) you might use when you have figured out exactly what you are trying to communicate, to whom, and against whom.

You cannot start to choose your marketing weapons until you have clarity about how you are trying to attract and with which method. Most marketing campaigns start with a budget and then select tools and then choose the message. This is a totally upside-down way of looking at the problem (unless you enjoy spending other people's money!).

The '*Customer Is King*' seven-point plan is a practical way of marrying the customer experience with the marketing of your business. If marketing is the 'promise' then operations is the delivery of the promise.

In a world where so many products tend to look similar (similar prices, features, staff, hardware, software) then the company that over-delivers on its promise... and understands why the customer wants what he/she wants... and is able to communicate this... will be the winner!

Assessing Your Weapons

Here's a tool to help you assess whether you have chosen the right marketing weapons for your business. Based loosely on the work of Levinson and McLaughlin, we did some qualitative research to understand how some of the key weapons performed for the average independent/ professional service firm.

Marketing Weapon	Level of Effort	£ Cost	Market Impact
Surveys	Medium-High	Medium-High	High
Special Reports	Medium	Medium	High
Newsletters/Ezines	Medium	Low	High
Speeches	Medium	Low	High
Books	High	High	High
Websites	Medium	Medium	Medium-High
Articles	Low-Medium	Low	Medium-High
Pro Bono Work	Low-medium	Low	Medium-High
Publicity	Medium	Low-Medium	Medium-High
Relationships/Networking	Medium-High	Low	Medium-High
Sponsored Events/trade Shows	Medium-High	Medium-High	Medium-High
Case Studies	Low	Low	Medium
Directory Listings	Low	Low	Medium
Direct Mail	Medium	Medium-High	Low-Medium
Printed Brochures	Medium	Medium-High	Low

The table shows you the relative level of effort, cost and impact of the most commonly used marketing weapons. You can add your own weapons and you can adjust the relative scores to fit your business and your industry score.

Consider the results for your business. Base your marketing spend (time and money) decisions on your desired impact and results. And test, test, test.

The 'Customer is King' system is an expert 'ology' – a true piece of BM thinking to help you grow your business sales and profits.

CUSTOMER EXPERIENCE

People talk about the 'customer experience' as if it is some magical, mystical event that is almost impossible to define. It doesn't seem that mysterious to me.

What Is The Customer Experience?

The customer experience is 'what you get' (referred to as 'Operations' in the FiMO exercise on page 34 and also a little more as well. Let me explain.

Operations is all about the delivery of the product or service – this is often seen from the producer's point of view:

- Are we giving them the right stuff?
- Are we giving them what they want?

The customer experience is that same transaction, except that it is seen through the eyes of the customer. So we ask:

'What does the transaction look like and feel like for the customer?'

Operations, as discussed earlier, does not operate in a vacuum. For the customer, a crucial element of receiving the product or service is whether it meets or exceeds expectations! If marketing is the promise and operations is the delivery of the promise, then the customer experience is where marketing meets operations!

Why Does the Customer Experience Matter?

I can't believe that I wrote that heading above. Of course it matters. It matters just about more than anything else!

The customer experience is probably the only thing that matters in your business. The customers pay the bills. The customers tell other people how great you are. Customers would rather be treated well than be treated badly. Customers remember exceptional service and tell others – they become your 'raving fans'. Customers remember dreadful service and tell others – that's the last thing that you need.

Question

If every company wants to delight its customers, then how come we don't spend most of our customer days delighted?

So What?

Providing legendary, remarkable service gets you talked about... and word-of-mouth marketing is one of the most powerful ways of 'spreading the word'.

Action Point

Score yourself on the table below. Just how good are you? How can you improve your score? What are you going to do to improve the customer experience that you deliver?

The Customer Experience

1. We stay 'close' at every stage of their experience

%
1 – 10 – 20 – 30 – 40 – 50 – 60 – 70 – 80 – 90 – 100
In your dreams   On a good day   Got it!

2. We create memorable 'wow!' encounters that inspire them to spread the legend to other potential customers.

3. We positively touch customers with the pride that we invest in our work.

4. We demonstrate superior levels of empathy for the customers' situation and needs.

5. We have created systems that are intuitively loved by customers – far more than just customer-friendly.

Providing an exceptional experience is the way to the customer's heart – don't just give them a transaction but let them build a relationship with you. This is digging into the emotional side of the relationship. Very powerful indeed.

THE BEST-KEPT SECRET ABOUT CUSTOMER SERVICE

Playing the devil's advocate, I'd like to present a view of customer service that is currently delivered by the big businesses. This is a little excursion; some mixed thoughts and ideas.

Key Point

It's harder to deliver good customer service than ever before, and yet, customers are more demanding.

A Question

Is the customer really in charge?

A Lie

The biggest lie today (as put out by marketing departments) is that 'the customer is in charge'.

Another Lie

Another lie is that 'customer service is better'. This simply isn't the case. Most people will tell you the reality is that most customer service is bad, very bad. Surely, everybody knows that!

So Why Do Big Businesses Try To Put The Customer In Charge?

The only reason to put the customer in charge is financial – costs for the business go down and… perceived service goes up because customers are doing the work themselves. In a world of imperfect customer service, most customers prefer to cut to the chase and help themselves (Think IKEA!).

Question

If every company wants to delight its customers, then how come we don't spend most of our customer days delighted? The reality is that customer service has reached the pits!

Stop and Think

As customers we feel betrayed. It seems remarkable that an entire business philosophy, a mantra, chanted across the modern world is so obviously without substance. Most businesses and organisations (be they hospitals, accountants, lawyers, airlines, universities, shops, restaurants, electrical retailers, broadband providers, builders' merchants, taxi firms, or software companies) blatantly fail to deliver. The customer is not king. The customer is left waiting to be heard (again!).

The reality is dismal. How often does the call centre tell you *'We are experiencing higher than usual call volumes'* or *'all our customer service operatives are currently busy'* or *'you are in a queue'*?

These statements are almost always followed by a second (incongruous) comment,
'We value your call'.

Grrrrrrrrrrrrr!!
If they value my call then why do I always have to wait?
If they are experiencing higher than usual call volumes then why don't we (the customers) experience higher than average staffing levels?

Smell the Coffee

Companies are starting to wake up to the fact that the customer is actually very angry with them. Customer service ratings are nonsense – after all, the average score is always 'above average'. (How does that work?)

So What?

Clearly, most customers do not feel 'in charge'. You can use this to your advantage – think how easy it can be to stand out from the rest when you really do put the customer in charge!

Meanwhile, How Real is Real?

So, how real is an 'Irish Pub' in Hampstead? Or home-made soup at the supermarket? We all hate feeling that we have been conned. And yet big businesses seem to be making a fortune by going out of their way to deliberately con us with contrivances and manipulations that are clearly false.

Real Relationships Blow Away The Sizzle Of Institutional Hype

There are huge opportunities for the independent-minded business in this world of mediocrity, of insipid service and lack of attention to the detail that really matters.

In just about every market, the dominance by the 'big boys' is resented. In their search for reliability, conformity and profitability they almost always forget about the customer (and the people that work at the business). Nine times out of 10, the local (and/or smaller) business may not be cheaper but can out-perform in terms of attention to service, detail, product knowledge, and customer understanding.

Large businesses cannot flex and respond and listen to the customer the way that a smaller business can. The energy and enthusiasm and excitement that a smaller business can generate (in staff and customers) can make the simplest shopping task quite pleasurable.

The question is whether you wish to rise to the challenge.

Success, What Success?

Success is a confusing thing for the growing business. You seek the popularity and profits that go with it; but then again, your product loses its intimacy with the success; your customers cease to get the individual attention that you were once able to give to them.

Stop and Think

If you hit upon a winning business formula, you have to make important choices. Should you expand, open another branch, franchise, license or what?

After all, if you've figured out a winning strategy, it seems only rational to cash-in by letting the market have what it wants: more of you! Let's play at devil's advocate for a moment. As long as you're giving the market what it wants, what's the problem? If some is good, then isn't more better?

The moment you take your special, authentic, limited-edition product and leverage it, make it widely available, the very people who loved it (also known as the 'early adopters' in marketing circles) will inevitably rebel.

'Starbucks isn't what it used to be,' they tell you. The early fans that made you successful in the first place turn on their heels when they smell that you're not authentic anymore. They say that 'before widespread popularity (ubiquity), when it seemed as if the product (or its creator) wasn't in it just for the money, somehow that felt more real, more wonderful, more authentic'.

Where Is All This Heading?

Enter the demon (or deity, depending on your point of view) called marketing. Brands, logos, salesmanship, positioning, and focus groups have become associated with corporate greed. It seems to be part of a game where 'they' are trying to win something over on 'us' (the consumer/customer). This mistrust of marketing comes from people's desire to have something real – and to get it from someone who isn't trying quite so hard to sell it.

Some Relevant Quotes

As Oscar Wilde says in *The Importance of Being Earnest*,

'In matters of grave importance, style, not sincerity, is the vital thing.'

Movie mogul Samuel Goldwyn once confessed,

'Sincerity's the main thing, and once you learn to fake that, everything else is easy.'

I saw the comedian Billy Connolly last month. A heckler called out:

'Tell us a joke, you rich ugly bastard.'

Connolly's reply was:

'If there's a choice between being rich and ugly, or poor and good-looking, then rich and ugly win every time.'

The Best-Kept Secret About Customer Service?

There are some basic things that we must not forget about customer service.

- First, service tends to be bad because it really is very hard to do.

- Second, the real (best-kept) secret is to treat the customer like you would like to be treated yourself.

- Third, the really hard part of providing excellent customer service is not the service! The really hard part is everything but the service! The hard part is to do with how the company thinks about what they are doing and how they behave as a consequence.

Most airlines offer bad service and bad food because they don't actually think of themselves as service organisations – they see themselves as machines for generating revenue per seat per mile. Most food outlets don't see themselves as service organisations – they see themselves as burger or pizza factories focusing on profit per employee per hour.

There is a huge opportunity out there waiting to be snatched up by the likes of you. Many people tolerate the mediocrity that seems to surround us. In fact, many people revel in the 'dumbing-down' that is all around us. An abundance of opportunities appear; opportunities to beat the big boys at their own game (because you are so much closer to your customer so you can give them a truly bespoke service). Opportunities to fill niches that the big boys are not interested in.

In Conclusion

Part Two: What Works – Tools For All *presented the tools that get used by nearly every business we work with – tools that you can't afford to miss*

Part Three: Other Tools – Help Yourself *offers a selection of tools, some of which you will find incredibly useful to help you to grow your business.*

PART THREE: OTHER TOOLS (HELP YOURSELF)

OTHER TOOLS

This part of the book offers a selection of tools, some of which you will find incredibly useful to help you to grow your business. I daresay that you may find that some of these tools are not suited specifically for your business. That's fine – you choose which tools you wish to use. Think of this section as a buffet or a box of chocolates – adopt a 'help yourself' approach and take as little or as much as you want!

Forrest Gump said 'My momma always said, "Life was like a box of chocolates. You never know what you're gonna get."'

THE MARKETING PACK

This chapter links back to the discussion on becoming seen as an expert (*THE EXPERT chapter*). Whatever type of promotional activity you are about to engage in, you need to produce a marketing pack.

This pack should contain all the bits and pieces you might need to present to:

- A potential customer
- A potential joint venture partner
- A new employee
- A web design company
- A journalist.

The process of putting the pack together will enable you to put your best foot forward – the pack itself will give the reader all the information that they need to understand what it is that you do and what makes you different from the rest. Interestingly enough, very few businesses actually go to the trouble of putting together such a 'pack'. The process of assembling the pack gets you to think through what you are trying to do with your marketing.

A typical pack might include some of the following, depending on your type of business and what is available:

- Testimonial letters from satisfied customers
- Celebrity endorsements
- Articles in which you're mentioned
- Published articles by you; unpublished articles by you; press releases
- A one- or two-page faxable flyer or printed trifold
- Audio/video cassettes/CDs/DVDs you've produced or been involved in
- Published 'New Product' announcements and/or press releases
- Copies of display advertisements
- Text from radio or TV advertisements
- A list of your memberships and affiliations
- Product catalogues, brochures, circulars, or data sheets

- Question-and-Answer sheets, FAQ (Frequently Asked Questions) sheets
- Annual report, capability statement, or prospectus
- Newsletters or news-type letters you use
- Your motto, mission statement, or service pledge
- Survey results by you or others
- Presentation notes, slides, or overheads
- Marketing letters you have written to clients
- Generic materials developed by your trade association
- Articles on trends affecting your target niche
- White Papers, Research Paper/Findings, How Tos by you
- Photos of your office facilities, equipment, products (with staff, clients, etc)… or photos of posters, banners, display materials used at trade shows
- Photos of you and your staff.

It is more than just a luxury to have a marketing pack ready to hand out at your fingertips. To have such a device/document demonstrates that you are serious about being in business and that you have taken the trouble to help others to really understand what it is that you do. A decent marketing pack will set you apart from the competition – very few people bother to take the time and effort to put one together.

WAYS TO GROW THE BUSINESS #1 – ANSOFF

I started my career as a sound recording engineer. The job became easy for me to understand when I was told that there were only two things you can do with sound in a recording studio: make it go up and down or make it go on and off.

In business there are only three new things you can do to grow a business:

1. **Change the product or service you deliver** (new product development: same market, new product).
2. **Change the markets you sell to** (market extension: new markets, same product)
3. **Combine the two** (diversification: new market, new product).

Number Four would be '*Do what you are already doing but do it better, faster, cheaper or quicker* (they call it '*market penetration*': same market, same product)' but that is not a new direction.

There is a tried and tested model used by many to analyse and develop market and product strategies for growing businesses developed by the management guru Igor Ansoff.

As depicted below, the Ansoff Matrix offers a logical framework to plot different strategies for growth.

Ansoff plotted two directions (market and product) on to axes and created a matrix framework to assess different strategies. In broad terms the four key strategic choices are:

1. New product development
2. Market extension
3. Diversification
4. Market penetration.

We've taken the standard two-by-two matrix and made it into a three-by-three matrix, which creates more options and permutations for using the tool.

Ansoff Matrix

Markets: Services / products:	Existing	Extension	New
Existing			
Modification			
New			

The Ansoff Matrix shows us possible opportunities that your business can pursue. The matrix reveals that there are levels of risk attached to any new direction.

There are levels of lesser and greater risk that can be drawn as you move away from the top left-hand corner of the matrix. Like isobars on a weather map, the risk increases as you move away from the 'comfort zone'. The matrix shows that the levels of risk increase as you move towards the bottom right-hand corner. So, make sure that you have really thought through the consequences of your potentially higher risk strategy.

How To Use It?

The bottom right-hand corner of the matrix often looks the most exciting and potentially profitable – it is also the most risky.

In the majority of cases, the most successful strategy is relatively uncomplicated. The highest risk strategy is *diversification* (new market, new product). Alarm bells ring when companies seek to combine the twin risks of entering new markets with new products. While this option seems very attractive, it may simply be an illusion.

In the cold light of day, companies that pursue the sexy (new product, new market), bottom right-hand corner *diversification* option are often ignoring the less sexy but safer top left-hand corner option of continuing to sell their existing product to their existing marketplace.

Checklist To Find Niches And Opportunities

1. *Neglected markets* where, say, customer needs have outpaced provision eg hand-built cars like *Morgan,* importing organic wines.

2. *Unfilled need* eg work away from office creates a demand for laptop computers, the creation of Pokemon card swapshops.

3. *Disadvantages in existing products* eg caffeine in coffee leads to decaffeinated coffee, short-life of cut flowers leads to demand for sachets containing long-life crystals for flower water.

4. *Omission in otherwise well-served markets* eg paper nappies, outdoor workers require robust mobile phones.

5. *Extensions or new formats for proven lines* eg T-shirts, scarves and sweatshirts for rugby supporters' club, Weight Watchers soups/Heinz.

6. *Technological breakthroughs* eg email-driven mentoring and business-support, special covers for reducing mobile phone radiation, bagless vacuum cleaners.

7. *Transferable success from other markets* eg yo-yo from Hawaii, tapas bar from Spain.

8. *More economical ways of satisfying wants now being met expensively:* temporary office accommodation, freelance IT managers that you buy in for a day or so a month.

9. *Less economical ways of satisfying wants that are being met only adequately:* Ben & Jerry's ice-cream, designer tailored football boots.

10. *Copy substitutes:* copy the competitive offering eg Wild Oats copied theme pubs and made board games and newspapers available in the restaurant, local delicatessen starts sandwich round to maintain sales.

11. *Do the opposite of traditional industry norms to emphasise the difference* Gerry Bentley adopted a 'pen and ink' approach to all communications in the face of database-driven and computer communications that his competition were using; chef Andreas Honore serves all meals to the tables of his restaurant guests.

12. *Change the product appeal and/or reinventing yourself* eg Lucozade changes itself from being a sick person's drink to being a healthy person's fitness drink, View

from move from satisfying mass market to appealing to professional athletes.

13. *Change the use of the product* eg isopropyl alcohol branded as video tape head cleaner and sold at 10 times higher price, bicarbonate of soda packaged and branded as refrigerator cleaner.

14. *Add complementary products or services* eg CD shops selling books and merchandise to complement CDs available, dentist selling generalist and specialist toothbrushes.

And in Practice...

A California-based retail computer company that specialised in selling PCs to the home market attempted to sell very expensive mainframe computers to large corporate organisations. This was a strategy that sent the company straight to the bottom right-hand corner of the Ansoff Matrix. Within three months it was in the insolvency courts. They simply did not realise how different the new offering was from the old one. Because they were both computers they (incorrectly) assumed that the same skills would be required to sell them, but the types of buyers and their needs were totally different as was the product and its features.

And in practice...

Web design and SEO (search engine optimisation agency) *MisterWeb* spent three years developing and nurturing website design for growing businesses and had grown to employ 23 coders and account managers. The owner-manager, Phil, had always had a potential business partnership lined up for a start-up web-based business for the air-conditioning industry (of which he had no experience). Spending roughly half a day a week on the new project, Phil finally realised several things:

- The start-up was really bottom right-hand corner of the Ansoff Matrix and therefore high-risk
- There was more than enough money to be made by systematically sticking to the top left-hand corner of the matrix.

Action Point

1. Looking at your business's growth to date, plot your business growth according to the growth matrix. Has your business growth been by product development or by market development, or by focusing in that bottom right-hand box? Have there been lots of little incremental steps on the way or big quantum leaps? How have you coped with and managed this type of change?

2. Looking at your business plans and options for the future, do they continue the trend to date? What is the consequence for managing the growth? How are you going to grow the business and what is the associated risk? If there are a series of choices to be made, then you can compare the different options using the matrix.

Marketing strategy is about trade-offs and choice – the growth matrix may help you to make those tough decisions.

Several people have observed that my enthusiasm for business school models is not huge. However, Ansoff changed my life! It was only when I was shown the Ansoff Matrix that I could make sense of my earlier business failures and successes.

WAYS TO GROW THE BUSINESS #2 - THE MULTIPLIER EFFECT

One of the top questions we are asked at the *BM* seminars is, 'How do I grow the business?' The session in the workshop on growing your business is always a fascinating one. Here we look at the 'Three Plus One' multiplier tool – it sounds very grand doesn't it!

Why Should I Care?

If you do the maths on the Three Plus One multiplier then you see how relatively small changes in activity can have massive effects on your business growth

Amaze Me!

There are three basic levers that you can manipulate to grow your business:

1. You can **get new customers.**
2. You can **get customers to buy more** (increased average order value).
3. You can **get customers to buy more often** (increased order frequency.

Combine these three levers and the effect really is very impressive!

More... More... More...
Ways to grow a business

■ **More customers** – get new customers

■ **More sales/customers** – get them to buy more (increase average order value)

■ **More sales/year** – get them to buy more often (increase order frequency)

One – Get New Customers

Get new customers always seems like the obvious way to grow the business but it is also a very expensive way to do so. Research suggests that it is between seven and 20 times more expensive to sell to a new customer than it is to sell to an existing customer. Acquiring new customers can be a very costly affair and you need to know how much it costs you to acquire a new customer so that you can start to work out how much it costs to acquire 10 new customers etc etc.

Two – Get Customers to Buy More

If you can, sell more to existing customers. Salesmen call this the 'upsell'. Is there any way that you can get people to buy additional items when they are purchasing from you? If they are buying a cake can you get them to buy a coffee as well? If they are buying a seat on a training programme, could you get them to buy a DVD as well? If they are buying a kitchen knife, could you get them to buy a knife sharpener as well? If they are buying roebuck shoes, could you get them to buy special roebuck shoe cleaner as well? I am sure that you've got the point.

Three – Get Customers To Buy More Often

The third lever in growing the business is to get people to buy more often. Can you get them into your store or to your website more often? This can have a dramatic impact on your sales volumes. Clearly, if you offer a one-off purchase (like funerals!) or occasional purchases (like divorces!) then it will be harder to sell more often to existing customers! However, in many cases there are opportunities to shorten the sales cycle so that you get more often.

For instance, in a restaurant you can run special theme evenings (Greek, Spanish, French, Halloween) to get existing customers to come more often. Or you can have a loyalty card that encourages and ultimately rewards regular visits.

The Impact of the Three Levers

The dramatic approach to growing the business is to see the impact of doubling all three levers.

So the questions are:

- Could you get each customer to refer you to one new client? This would double your number of clients
- Could you get existing customers to buy twice as much? This would double turnover
- Could you get them to buy twice as often? This would also double turnover.

In this over-simplified example...

- A company with 100 customers
- With an average transaction value of £100 and
- Five sales per customer per year
- Turning over £50,000 (100 x £100 x 5).

Would become...

- A company with 200 customers
- With an average transaction value of £200 and
- Ten sales per customer per year
- Turning over £400,000 (200 x £200 x 10).

This is an eightfold increase in turnover.

More... More... More...
Quick 'n' dirty

- **More customers** – get each client to get you ONE new client!

- **More sales/customers** – sell TWICE as much to each client...

- **More sales/year** – get them to buy TWICE as often

100 x £100 x 5 = £50,000
200 x £200 x 10 = £400,000!!!

While the quick and dirty approach gives ridiculously impressive results, it is worth considering the impact of more realistic changes.

For most businesses, you should be able to
- Increase the number of customers by, say, 5%
- Increase the average transaction value by, say, 5%
- Increase the number of sales per year by, say, 5%.

The impact of these relatively small changes is still pretty dramatic.

In this over-simplified example...
- A company with 100 customers
- With an average transaction value of £100 and
- Five sales per customer per year
- Turning over £50,000 (100 x £100 x 5).

This would become...
- A company with 105 customers
- With an average transaction value of £105 and
- 5.25 sales per customer per year
- Turning over £57,880 (105 x £105 x 5.25).
This is a 16% increase in turnover – pretty good for a few small improvements.

More... More... More...
Results

	start	add 5%	add 10%	add 25%	add 50%	add 100%
Customers (no.)	100	105	110	125	150	200
Sales/cust (£)	£100	£105	£110	£125	£150	£200
Sales/year (no.)	5	5.25	5.5	6.25	7.5	10
Turnover	£50,000	£57,881	£66,550	£97,656	£168,750	£400,000
	100%	116%	133%	195%	338%	800%

When we work through this example to find the result on profit we see that the three 5% changes result in a massive 43% increase in net profit!

And The 'Plus One'?

The 'Plus One' is the factor that people always seem to forget about. The 'Plus One' is the customers that leave us – the technical name would be 'customer attrition rate'.

The statistics are simply amazing...
- 5% of customers leave us because they die – fair enough!
- 5% of customers leave us because they 'die gracefully' – they move on, the business closes down, they go into partnerships, etc
- 5% of customers leave us because of our bad service
- 65% of customers leave us because they feel that we don't care; they feel that we are pretty indifferent to them and so they move on to someone who does care about them and is keen to have their business!

Out of Interest...

When was the last time that you did a customer survey? Because if you haven't done one very recently, then how do you know what they are thinking?! And if you don't know what they are thinking about you and your business, then maybe they are thinking of moving on.

You must stay close to your customers so that you make them think that you are not indifferent to them!!!

I hate the way that certain consultants bandy around incredible numbers that demonstrate how you can double your profits in three weeks, or whatever the latest claim is that is used to try to win over customers. Having said that, it is incredible that relatively small changes in the Three Plus One system can have tremendous results on your business performance. My advice is apply the tool yourself – don't be fooled by the smoke, mirrors and snake oil that is sold as helping your business – you have been warned.

THE FASTSTRAT FOUR-PAGER – A FAST AND EFFECTIVE PLANNING PROCESS TO USE

Over the last five years we have been using what we have come to call FastStrat worksheets for quick and dirty (but effective) plans for the business. Such a great yet simple tool to help you to run a better business.

Instructions

Spend roughly half an hour on each of the following worksheets.

FastStrat1: How To Raise Client Satisfaction?

How can you make your customers happier? Because the happier they are...

- The more they'll be happy to pay
- The more people they will tell about you
- The more they will forgive you if you screw up
- The more you will enjoy working with them.

FastStrat2: How To Increase Skill-Building?

The better your skills then the better you are at:

- Delegating
- Selling
- Negotiating
- Leading, and
- Delighting the client!

FastStrat3: How To Improve Productivity?

Better productivity means:

- You get more stuff through the business in the same amount of time or it takes you less time to do the same amount of stuff
- More effectiveness
- More efficiency
- More profit
- More cash.

FastStrat4: How To Get Better Business?

Before you can decide how to get better business you need to decide what better business is for your business – is it business:

- Within 25 miles?
- More than £1,000 per order?
- From blue-chip companies?
- Repeat business?

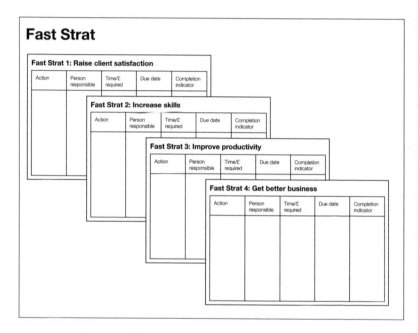

I cannot talk highly enough of the four FastStrat worksheets. We use them regularly in our own business and recommend them to almost every client that we work with.

FIVE BY FIVE (5x5)

The Five By Five (5x5) is another one of our favourite worksheets.

When Do You Use It?

This is a great worksheet for delegates to use at the end of a workshop as a way of bringing together the actions that you are going to put in place to make sure that you see results from your attendance.

And Why Should You Use It?

Using the worksheet gets you to think through, and commit to paper, some key decisions. It is better than the more vague worksheets that are often used (eg 'What are you going to do as a result of today?' or 'What part of the course did you find most useful?') as it actually drills down to activities that you should or ought to be taking. As a delegate, you focus on actions and outcomes and outputs rather than nice soft, touchy feely 'to do' lists. I love it.

Five By Five

- **Five tasks I want to finish (but haven't)**

- **Five decisions I want to make**

- **Five ways I want to maximise my time**

- **Five new connections I want to make**

- **Five big steps I want to make**

Action Points

Fill in the gaps...

■ Five tasks I want to finish (but haven't)
[eg re-sorting the database... Action: get Jo to finish it by next Thursday]

1. ....
2. ....
3. ....
4. ....
5. ....

■ Five decisions I want to make
[eg Move to a new accountant... Action: get recommendations from colleagues and visit potential new accountants, say four, within next 14 days in order to make a decision within 21 days]

1. ....
2. ....
3. ....
4. ....
5. ....

■ Five ways I want to maximise my time
[eg stop wasting my time when I have employees working for me... Action: delegate all tasks that don't need to be done by me; train staff and show them what to do and how to do it... by next Friday]

1. ....
2. ....
3. ....
4. ....
5. ....

■ Five new connections I want to make
[eg find out the name of the business editor of the local paper and offer to take him/her to lunch]

1. ....
2. ....
3. ....
4. ....
5. ....

■ Five big steps I want to take
[eg appoint a non-executive director within three months (if a suitable person is available)]

1. ....
2. ....
3. ....
4. ....
5. ....

This process of mapping out what it is that you want to do is a great way to focus your activities on things that have been blocking your progress.

PSF 2010

Tom Peters, (Management Consultant who set up tompeters! company , a management consultancy and training firm), in his recent work, has spoken a lot about the PSF (Professional Service Firm). His work is challenging yet inspirational, and his ideas and thoughts are always worth reading.

When looking at how the PSF might behave in 2010 Tom Peters came up with a series of key ideas that are crucial to the growth of the business and can be encapsulated as follows:

High Value-Added Projects

You should only be doing projects that really do add value to the client, over and above the standard norm. Clients will return if you 'go the extra mile'; they will not tolerate you doing 'just enough'. Just enough is never good enough for you or for them!

Pioneer Clients

Don't just work with the easy clients where you do repeat work that you have done before. It is the challenging clients that really push you and get you to think about the solutions you are offering; this will improve the quality of your work. They may not be so easy to deal with, and you may hate them at times, but pioneer clients will stretch you to come up with unique solutions that other practitioners won't have considered. And all this can be fed back into your everyday work!

'Wow' Work

At its simplest you need to be doing work that blows away your clients – if they don't think that you are delivering 'wow' work, but just ordinary bog-standard run-of the-mill stuff, then they may well spend their money elsewhere next time!

Hot 'Talent'

Employ the best if you want the best results. The saying goes, 'if you pay peanuts then you get monkeys'! Recently a (small) client said that they really wanted to grow the business so they literally sought out a 'world-class' managing director to take the business to the next level. And it worked!

Adventurous Culture

Culture can be defined as how we do things around here. So how do you do things in your business? Is there a culture of adventure or is it all 'business as usual'? Just how exciting is it to work in your business or to come into your business as a client?

Proprietary Point Of View (PPOV)

You need an 'ology', a way of doing things that belongs to you – you need it so that you have a systematic, measured approach to your work; your clients need it so that they have a sense of what it is that you do, how you do it and a sense of your uniqueness!

Work Worth Paying For

Heaven forbid that you ever do any work that is not worth paying for because that is the time to stop, pack up your bags and go home. We must only ever do work worth PAYING for!

And when should this happen?

NOW!

Score Yourself

Score yourself on a scale of 1 – 10 where '1' means 'never' and '10' means 'all the time'.

	Never	All the time
We do 'High Value-Added Projects'	1 2 3 4 5 6 7 8 9 10	
We have 'Pioneer Clients'	1 2 3 4 5 6 7 8 9 10	
We do 'Wow Work'	1 2 3 4 5 6 7 8 9 10	
We employ 'Hot Talent'	1 2 3 4 5 6 7 8 9 10	
We have an 'Adventurous Culture'	1 2 3 4 5 6 7 8 9 10	
We have a 'Proprietary Point Of View (PPOV)'	1 2 3 4 5 6 7 8 9 10	
We do 'Work Worth Paying For'	1 2 3 4 5 6 7 8 9 10	

So...

What can you do to create a better PSF? List five things right now.

And in Practice

The board of JWT, an internet marketing agency employing 125 staff, felt that the whole business had become stale and had lost the entrepreneurial sparkle, verve and excitement that it had when it was smaller. Everything had become a grind and, to be honest, they were churning out a lot of mediocre work to some pretty unremarkable and unchallenging clients.

With their hands on their hearts the board could not give themselves a score of more than five for any of the criteria in the PSF 2010 chart above. This was a sad moment – a time to admit that they had sat back and allowed their need for security to exceed their need for excitement.

As the MD euphemistically said, 'decisions were made to liven things up'. A few staff left but on the whole everyone loved the new adventure to push the scores on the chart as far to the right as possible.

This was not just some silly exercise to make things more fun; in fact, for 'fun' read the word 'risky'. With their new focus on the PSF 2010, they started to seek more challenging clients and more challenging work which started to separate them out from the competition, and it allowed them to do more perilous but more profitable work. Their reputation blossomed and so did their order book (up 35% on the previous year).

The PSF 2010 list gets all sorts and types of businesses to think about how they approach the market. It does focus on the gap between 'the promise' (marketing) and 'the delivery' (operations). *See the HOW AM I DOING? HOW GOOD IS MY MARKETING? chapter.*

STRANGERS, FRIENDS AND LOVERS – UPSIDE-DOWN MARKETING!

Conventional wisdom isn't always so clever – sometimes it helps to turn it upside-down!

I divide the world of clients and potential clients into four simple-to-understand categories:

- **Strangers** – the broader market, they don't know who I am
- **Friends** – prospective clients we've met, they know who I am, but they haven't bought from us so we aren't that close yet!
- **Lovers** – current clients who love us, and, of course,
- **Ex-lovers** – ex-clients, who have fallen out of love with us!

Conventional Wisdom
Most marketers budget their time and financial expenditure as follows:

- 60% – Strangers
- 30% – Friends
- 10% – Lovers.

In other words, they spend most of their marketing effort focusing on people they don't really know.

Conventional Wisdom Turned Upside-Down
It seems mad to spend most of your time and money on people who don't even know who you are. It makes no sense at all. Any betting person would prefer to bet where there's the best chance of getting a result. So, I suggest that you should consider what would happen if you spent your marketing budget as follows:

- 10% – Strangers
- 30% – Friends
- 60% – Lovers.

This way you spend most of your effort with people who already think that you are great – they already love you. A

And by spending more time and effort with them, they will spread the word. They can act as your ambassadors, your 'raving fans'. They know your strengths and weaknesses; they can help your business by spreading the word or giving you warm referrals. Think about it.

Spend a little time considering this piece of upside-down thinking – in the right business this process will increase your marketing effectiveness tremendously.

THE SALES/ PROSPECTING FUNNEL – CUSTOMER RELATIONSHIPS AND PIPELINES

The sales or prospecting funnel is a tool that many have never come across and others are totally obsessed with. You are definitely missing a trick if you don't use such a device – this is a tool that will improve your ability to win new clients.

One of the prevailing questions about marketing goes something like:
'I understand all the theory and how to put a strategy and sales plan together but how do you make it happen? What tools or devices do you need to track and monitor what you are doing?'

Enter 'The Sales Funnel'. In fact, enter the *Bright Marketing* Sales Funnel™. OK, I jest about the trademark sign but anyone who has ever shown me a marketing funnel or pipeline covers it with all kinds of trademark and copyright signs as if they are showing the world something that belongs exclusively to their own intellectual property. What utter nonsense.

So What is the Sales Funnel?

In essence, imagine a funnel. At the top of the funnel are all the people you could work with (leads). Out of the bottom of the funnel drop all the people you will work with (clients). To progress along the funnel they need to move through various stages of your sales cycle from prospect to possible client.

In the previous chapter (page number 125) I talked about the stages of my relationships; people were either:

■ Strangers
■ Friends
■ Lovers
■ Ex-lovers.

This way of dividing up the world is incredibly helpful in terms of understanding what the world consists of and it also helps me to understand who I am, or should be, talking to.

As a different way of examining the world, we use a similar model but now we divide people up by the stage and type of relationship that we have.

As clients get progressively closer to us, going through the stranger-friend-lover stages they go through a series of stages and activities.

Most clients go through each of the following stages to become a client...

- Lead — strangers
- Conversation — friends
- Proposal — friends
- Client — lovers.

At first they are a **lead** — they have come across us and seen our business card, advert or website...

Then, they have a **conversation** with us — we talk about how our product or service may suit their needs...

Next, they ask for and they are given a **proposal** — we quote them for a piece of work...

Finally, they become a **client** — they buy from us.

Next Steps

You can start to calculate how many people move from one stage to the next.

If you have, say, 800 visitors to your website (leads) then maybe 50% of those people start a dialogue with you (a conversation) to discuss how you might be able to help them. Of those 400 conversations maybe 50% of the people ask for a proposal or a quote. Of the 200 proposals that you present them with, maybe 50 of them turn into clients at an average rate of £x each. With time you will know the numbers and the probabilities to predict how many people from each stage should finally end up as clients.

So the questions you must ask yourself are:

- Could you be better at getting **leads**?
  - Of course you could — do more networking, more adverts, talk to more people

- Could you be better at your **conversations** with potential clients?
  – Of course you could – go on a sales course or personal development course or one on body language
- Could you be better at writing **proposals**?
  – Of course you could
- Could you be better at converting people from the proposal stage to becoming **clients**?
  – Of course.

The impact of small improvements at each stage of the sales funnel has quite dramatic effects. Just a 10% improvement at each stage creates a 46% increase in your success rate of converting leads to become clients! (Small changes accumulate to create big results.)

Moving stuff along the sales pipeline

	Current situation	Change	New situation
Leads	800	add 10%	880
Conversion of leads to conversations	50%	add 10%	55%
Conversations	400		484
Conversion of conversations to proposals	50%	add 10%	55%
Number of proposals	200		266
Proposal success rate	50%	add 10%	55%
Successful proposals	100		146
			46%

The sales funnel is one of the key tools that is in place in a successful, growing business. Understanding the potential customer's journey and the steps that they need to go through (and measuring and tracking the number of potential customers at the different stages) enables you to put processes in place that make sure that you speed up the cycle-time and don't lose anyone because you weren't on top of the situation.

CUSTOMER FUNDAMENTALS

I first saw a very similar list to the one below when the internet first got going. While some of the technology may have moved on a bit since 1998, Patricia Seybold (Management and e-commerce guru, founder and CEO of the Patricia Seybold Group, a strategic e-business and consultancy firm) really did hit the mark when she talked about the customer fundamentals that we should never forget.

For simplicity's sake, I have reproduced Patricia Seybold's 'laws' in the form of a slide.

Customer fundamentals

- ■ Don't waste our time
- ■ Remember who we are
- ■ Make it easy for us to order and get service
- ■ Make sure your service delights us!
- ■ Customise your products and services

CREATING A USP

We are often asked how to create a 'USP'. USP is one of those ghastly management buzzwords that seem to mean everything and nothing.

The concept of the USP ('Unique Selling Point' or 'Unique Selling Proposition') was very fashionable in marketing and MBA circles in the 1980s. It seems a little out of favour now, which is a shame really as it is a great tool to get you thinking about what makes your business different from the rest. In fact the USP is, in many ways, a forerunner of the one-minute logo/ elevator pitch/audio logo (*see ONE-MINUTE INTRO chapter*).

What Is It?
USP was once the way to define what makes you unique.

Is It Now Redundant?
Far from it. It is a great tool to get you and your business colleagues to define what makes you different from the rest.

How Does It Work?
Most people have had an issue about finding a process to identify their USP. Below are the worksheets we use to get people to understand their USP.

So, in essence, you fill in the gaps in the sheets:

- You know how some companies/competitors do...
- Which means that...
- Well, what we do is...
- Which means that...

And in Practice – Let Me Give You An Example
- **You know how some training companies...**
  claim to make everything bespoke but really they just change the logo on the workbooks...
- **Which means that...**
  you feel ripped off and don't get a unique product...
- **Well, what we do is...**
  spend a day in your business so we understand what you really need (rather than what you want)...

■ **Which means that...**
   you get a training programme that absolutely fits your needs.

And in Practice – Another Example

■ **You know how some business speakers...**
   are full of academic rhetoric
■ **Which means that...**
   you get bored stupid by their clever clogs theories about
   running a business...
■ **Well, what we do is...**
   only talk about things that we have done in our own
   business...
■ **Which means that...**
   you get ideas which are 100% based in the real world.

Creating a USP   sheet #1

You know how some companies struggle to find a supplier who:

....

....

Which means that:

....

....

Creating a USP   sheet #2

Well, what we do is:

....

....

Which means that:

....

....

---

*The USP may not be a new concept and it may
not be possible for everyone to have a genuinely
unique product. It is, however, a worthwhile
exercise to challenge your thinking to develop an
understanding of what makes your offering different
from the rest (and to use/exploit that knowledge).*

THE INFLUENCERS CHART

The Influencers Chart is one of those tools that gets mentioned at our workshops – it is not one of the 'BIG' tools but it is one that a lot of people find incredibly powerful.

What Is It?
The Influencers Chart is a tool that gets you to think about:
- Who you know and how influential they are in helping your business?
- Who you know and how committed they are to helping your business?
- What actions you can take to get these people working for you?

How Does It Work?
1) List say 20 people you know.
2) Write down a percentage score for how committed they are to helping your business.
3) Write down a percentage score for how influential they could be in helping your business.
4) Action: who are the really influential people, the people who are influential and committed to helping you? Who should you get to be more committed? Who should you be talking to and arranging meetings with? Write down the actions that you need to take.

The Influencers Chart

Name	How committed %	How influential %	Action

Not a 'BIG' tool indeed... However, it is still a great tool for getting you to re-think who is and who should be on your side and how you might be able to get more powerful/influential people on to your side.

In Conclusion

Part Three: Other Tools – Help Yourself provided a further selection to the tools provided in Part Two – What Works – Tools For All, some of which you will find incredibly useful to help you to grow your business (while some may not be so appropriate for your particular business!).

Part Four will go on to introduce the Bright Marketing Manifesto.

PART FOUR:
A BRIGHT
MARKETING
MANIFESTO

MANIFESTO

In this final Part Four, we bring together the *BM* 'ology' in a series of Laws, Crunch Questions, and the Manifesto itself. Part Two and Three gave you the *BM* tools, the 'what' and 'how' of the *BM* toolkit. This final part contains the key documents that help you to understand how the *Bright Marketing* 'ology' comes together.

THE IMMUTABLE LAWS OF MARKETING

Here are what I consider to be the immutable laws of marketing – 16 Laws that help you to understand why you are (or are not) successful in your efforts to attract and retain customers...
The Immutable Laws Of Customer-Focused Marketing (For New And Growing Businesses).

The immutable laws of marketing demonstrate to new and to growing businesses (or any other business for that matter) that need plain, common sense and no-nonsense marketing help. They were assembled with the assistance of my friend and colleague, Timothy Cumming. They appear in no particular order.

The 16 Immutable Laws of Customer-Focused Marketing (For New And Growing Businesses)...

1. The Law Of Perception
2. The Law Of Questions
3. The Law of Precision
4. The Law Of Different Missions For Different Positions
5. The Law Of Time
6. The Integration Law
7. The Law Of The Driving Seat
8. The Law Of Measurement
9. The First Law
10. The Law Of Tricky Extensions
11. Pareto's Law
12. The Laws Of Success And Failure
13. The Law Of Reversibility
14. The 'P-FAB-P' Law
15. The Law Of PLC
16. The Law Of The KISS

1 The Law Of Perception
Marketing is a battle of perceptions and not simply a battle of products.

Most people seem to assume that, in the battle for customers, it is the best product that wins. This is clearly not the case. The winner is the product that customers believe to be the best as proven by whether they buy or not.

While the product's quality or features may play an important part in the buyer's decision-making process, there are many forms of persuasion which will have influenced thinking – brand image, company reputation, or competitor comparisons to name but a few, and all of these are perception. The job in hand is to win over the customer's mind.

2 The Law Of Questions
Questions lead to answers; answers lead to relationships; relationships lead to profit.

One of the easiest ways to put the customer first is to ask questions (and to respect the customer's answers!) The more you ask, the more competitive advantage you gain, and the stronger your customer relationships become. To make the customer feel in control, ask the right questions to find what they want from you.

3 The Law Of Precision
The ability to accurately define your precise market segments dramatically affects your profitability. So segment carefully!

Divide your markets into slices that are distinctive, profitable and which suit your strengths. Ditch the rest and really concentrate on just those segments. It'll save you money on promotion and production/operations and will strengthen your sales messages. Figure out whom you can really delight.

4 The Law Of Different Missions For Different Positions
Your strategies depend upon your position.

If you fail to be Number One in the prospect's mind then you have to adopt different strategies. In the Number Two position, you must differentiate yourself from the Number One; otherwise you just look like a pale imitation.

The best way to separate yourself is to focus on the differences, the opposites.

eg 'We are professional and thorough so sometimes things will take a little longer – it's worth the wait', 'If you don't want to be treated like a number...', 'We offer fixed price packages' and so on.

Use the appropriate strategy for your position.

5   The Law Of Time

Marketing returns exist in the long-term.
Be aware that short-term gains (sales today) may be at the cost of the longer-term game. Your 'offer' must be consistent and it must be consistently consistent. A sale price may imply that you are over-charging at other times – the result is reduced future sales at the premium rates as punters wait for the next sale offer.

Be aware of the relationship between the long-term and the short-term. Short-term gains seem fine, but at what cost? Decide your goals and be prepared to pay the price (probably in advance)!

6   The Integration Law

Marketing is nothing if it is not company-wide.
If the marketing or sales people are the only ones carrying the marketing flag, you're in trouble! Customers will read your marketing messages as loose promises and hot air if the reality isn't as glittering as the claims. Plan and relate the marketing aspects of every business activity for the whole company.

Educate your production/operations people, your office manager and your receptionist so that they understand their role in putting the customer first.

7   The Law Of The Driving Seat

The management team is the centre for improvement.
You won't pull off miraculous improvements from anywhere else! Drive all your marketing programmes from the management team. Get everybody involved – but make

it your priority to drive the programme from the top. Otherwise other priorities will take over, practical hurdles will get in the way and your marketing development will sink in a swamp of mediocrity.

8 The Law of Measurement

Don't just measure – Interpret.
Sure, measure all you can – an objective isn't worth the paper it's written on if you can't track your progress towards it. But don't be a bean-counter. Analyse the results – interpret them for meaningful trends or comparisons. A '48% increase in demand for after-sales care' may be interpreted as 'the product needs tweaking, and clients want stronger relationships'.

9 The First Law

If you aren't Number One in your existing category then create your own category, or be the first in their minds.
People love to buy from Number One in the category; they believe that Number One is better than the rest (otherwise why would they be Number One?). So you can always be 'Best in the West', 'The First Mexican Takeaway', the 'Original One-Stop Shop', the 'Only Printers With A Money-Back Guarantee' and so forth. If customers love the leader then find a way to lead.

But all is not lost if you can't be first in category. With a simpler name to remember or a new product (better, quicker, cheaper, faster, or nicer) suddenly you've taken poll position in their minds. It is amazing how the mind allows only two or three names to be associated with a product or service. That's why new names can knock one of the older and less 'active' big names off the top of list, suddenly becoming a household name (Dyson cleaners are a prime example). If the new kid on the block can make a lasting impression then they may be able to steal a march on the so-called 'old and trusted'. Big names be warned – we live in a changing world and you cannot afford to rest on your laurels, especially if you've been at the top of the league for some time.

10 The Law Of Tricky Extensions

The irresistible urge to extend product lines or move into new markets may be self-defeating in the long run – 'brand equity', when stretched, usually gets spread more thinly.

A good brand and reputation for one product or service doesn't necessarily extend to a new range or market. Some brands can do it – and at what price? And others cannot. Be aware of just how difficult it is to do something you are not really expert in and don't kid yourself otherwise.

A café by day thinks it can do outside catering or posh evening meals; a delicatessen thinks it can run a sandwich round. When you go into a new market or product area you just 'don't know what you don't know' – always assess the opportunity rationally. (See the Ansoff Matrix.)

11 Pareto's Law

The 80/20 Rule is everywhere – to be effective, cut back on the ineffective and focus on the effective efforts. (It's also everywhere in this book!)

Pareto's 80/20 Principle is everywhere we look: 80% of profits come from 20% of customers; 80% of sales come from 20% of the sales force; and, conversely 20% of sales would generate 80% of profit. If you want to work smarter, focus on the highly effective and ignore the rest!

Draw a line below your Top 20% of clients and inform the rest of new prices to give you margins similar to those with the profitable clients. Some will 'play the game' which is fine and some will not which is fine also because you don't want their business in the first place. Who wants to be a busy fool?

So, find out the characteristics of your top 20% and find some more customers like them.

12 The Laws Of Success And Failure

Success and failure go hand-in-hand – it's OK to make mistakes but you must learn from them; and... remember, nothing succeeds like success.

Failure is part of learning; if you didn't fail occasionally then you couldn't be taking enough risks. Recognise a failure and cut your losses before disaster ensues. It is only the 'English way' that is so unforgiving of business failure; how else do you find out if an idea can work if you don't experiment? The issue is the price that you might have to pay.

Success can be as damaging as failure. Healthy bank balances and being Number One in league tables make organisations arrogant, big-headed and sluggish; they start to believe in their myths. Then the competition move in and steal the action.

You are at your most vulnerable when you are Number One; everyone wants to knock you off your perch and will be willing to undercut your prices to win some work away from you. Customers start to use you as a reference point but might be able to buy a similar-looking product at a lower price.

13 The Law Of Reversibility

Start with the end in mind, and accept responsibility for the results.

If you start with your end in mind then you are able to picture the stepping-stones to getting there; looking back from the visualised scenario you can see what will need to be done. This is a far more productive way of planning the future as it points out all the potential hurdles along the way. It also focuses the mind on cause and effect. Remember, there are reasons why customers will buy or refuse your products and services. Understand that you can determine the effects that you want but that this requires dedication and planning.

14 The 'P-FAB-P' Law

Customers buy benefits and proofs – show them the advantages and features but make sure the benefits and proofs address their problem.

See things through the customers' eyes. As the saying goes, if you want to understand a Red Indian, spend a day walking in his/her moccasins. When looking through the customers' eyes always think 'What's in it for me?' (WIIFM?). 'P-FAB-P' refers to Problem, Features, Advantages, Benefits and Proofs. As producers we get pre-occupied with what we put into the product (ie the features). Customers are much more interested in what is in it for them (they focus on benefits) and how we can demonstrate these benefits (the proofs). Every sales pitch should employ the words 'Which means that...' to ensure that you are explaining how your product will solve your customers' problem.

15 The Law Of PLC

The Product Life Cycle will haunt you in all your work.
Just about every product in the long run will go through a series of stages of growth (conception, birth, growing pains, development, adolescence, maturity and death). You can try to extend or re-invigorate any particular phase but the law will not go away. Understanding that the law exists enables you to design your strategy to reflect or resist the current stage that you are in.

Remember also the difference between a fad and a trend – fads tend to be short-lived (although the Law Of PLC suggests that a fad can return, albeit in a reincarnated state, in a cyclical fashion).

16 The Law Of The KISS

Keep It Simple Stupid
This was one of the reasons in the chapter on why marketing fails (page number 23)! Marketing can be hugely effective as long as you don't make it too clever or sophisticated – complexity does not help the customer.

You can use these 16 laws to help you improve your business – look at them one at a time, or as a whole, in order to help you to improve your marketing.

CRUNCH QUESTIONS

Crunch Questions – a brilliant list of questions for you to consider.

Take the Crunch Questions with you on, say, a train journey, and consider each one carefully – don't just answer the questions without thinking about the implications of your answers.

You may wish to ponder some of these questions quite carefully. The objective is not to answer the questions as quickly as possible. The purpose is to reflect on your answers and what they mean for your business.

1. What business are you really in?

....
....
....

2. Where do you make the money?

....
....
....

3. How good are your competitive positions?

....
....
....

4. Is this a good industry to be in?

....
....
....

5. What do your clients think?

....
....
....

6. How do you raise profits quickly?

....

....

....

7. How do you build long-term value?

....

....

....

8. What do you do differently from other businesses?

....

....

....

9. What investments underpin your differences?

....

....

....

10. What are your key sources of competitive advantage?

....

....

....

11. What do you need to do to make a difference?

....

....

....

12. What must you keep? What must you lose?

....

....

....

13. How could you simplify your business so that you could raise value-to-clients by at least 50%?

....

....

....

14. Isn't your strategy rather complex? Aren't all great strategies very simple?

....
....
....

15. What is the key idea, your business concept?

....
....
....

16. Who is your target client?

....
....
....

17. What do you really know about them?

....
....
....

18. Can you describe a typical client in detail?

....
....
....

19. What problem are you solving?

....
....
....

20. Why do people buy your product at all?

....
....
....

21. Why do people buy your product from you?

....
....
....

22. Why does your typical client buy from you?

....

....

....

23. Which clients are cool?

....

....

....

24. Which clients drive you mad?

....

....

....

25. Should you be working with them?

....

....

....

26. What benefits are you offering that your competition doesn't?

....

....

....

27. If you could use just two sentences to describe what your business stands for, what would they be?

....

....

....

28. What is your company known for?

....

....

....

29. What's your 'value proposition' to clients that they can't get anywhere else?

....

....

....

30. Who are your most profitable clients?

....

....

....

31. At what rate do they leave you?

....

....

....

32. Why do they leave?

....

....

....

33. Who is your most serious competitor?

....

....

....

34. What are their plans?

....

....

....

35. And what are their costs, profits?

....

....

....

36. Do you really know what clients think about you?

....

....

....

37. Who are currently just new/minor threats?

....

....

....

38. Are you supplying the right things?

....

....

....

39. And in the most effective way?

....

....

....

40. And at the lowest possible economic cost?

....

....

....

41. Are you as good or better than your best competitor?

....

....

....

42. Are you serving the widest possible market?

....

....

....

43. Are you in some way unique? Is there a reason why people should buy from you rather than from someone else?

....

....

44. Would God have a good laugh if he saw your marketing plan?

....

....

....

45. What keeps you awake at night about your business?

....

....

....

46. What are your objectives? What are you trying to achieve?

....

....

....

47. What will enable you to overcome the barriers, and/or achieve the objectives?

....

....

....

48. If you had a magic wand, what changes would you make to the business?

....

....

....

49. What is stopping you from making your magic wand changes now?

....

....

....

50. What three things are the most critical to the success of the business?

....

....

....

51. Which 20% of clients account for 80% of profit?

....

....

....

52. Who are your top five clients and how much contribution did they generate last month?

....

....

....

....

....

....

53. Which clients are unprofitable?

....

....

....

54. Which clients should you sack?

....

....

....

55. Which products/services should you raise the selling price on now?

....

....

....

56. Which under-performing products/services should you drop now?

....

....

....

57. Which products/services should you concentrate on selling more of?

....

....

....

58. What is success for you?

....

....

....

59. What is success for the business?

....

....

....

60. What does your business stand for?

....

....

....

61. Is the work you do exciting or dull?

....

....

....

62. So what is it that you do that is so exciting?

....

....

....

63. Does what you do matter?

....

....

....

64. How could you raise the impact?

....

....

....

65. Are you pushing or leading or goading your clients?

....

....

....

66. If your business were an animal, what would it be and why?

....

....

....

67. What animal would you wish your business to be and why?

....

....

....

68. What do you need to do to get your business from being the animal that it is, to become the animal that you wish it to be?

....

....

....

69. If your business were an island, what sort of island would it be?

....

....

....

70. Running your business is like riding a bicycle because…

....

....

....

71. If you could work half-time, what would you do to double your profit?

....

....

....

72. What would Sir Richard Branson do if he took over your business?

....

....

....

73. What would your closest rival do if they took over your business?

....

....

....

74. How can you get luckier?

....

....

....

75. What excuses do you tend to use?

....

....

....

I implore you to use these crunch questions to get you to focus on how you are going to get more and better clients and customers to buy from you.

SOME ONE-LINERS

Like the crunch questions, the one-liners are a great way to challenge your assumptions about how you do business. And the purpose of the one-liners is not just to be clever, but to get you to think about how to improve the way that you do business.

■ Brand It

You cannot not communicate your brand. Everything about your business communicates something. So, what is it that you want to be communicating? First decide what it is that you wish to communicate and to whom.

■ Brand YOU

Treat yourself like a business treats its brand. You need to plan and create a strategy for communicating what it is that you represent, what it is that you do, and where you want to be seen and what you want to be known for. What is your Unique Selling Point (USP)?

■ Keep It

Don't make changes for the sake of it. If it ain't broke, don't fix it. We spend too much time recreating, re-engineering things that are perfectly okay.

■ Get Your Clients' Permission To Sell To Them

Traditional mass-selling techniques are simply not effective and have low success rates. Look for clients to give you permission to stay in contact with them. Clients who have given you permission to have a relationship with them are 10 times more likely to spend money with you.

■ People Love To Buy From People, But They Hate To Be Sold At

In today's one-to-one marketing world, clients hate to be *sold at* by badly trained salesmen. But, clients love *to buy* products *from* you. Seduce them to your business but do not treat them like morons.

■ Strategy Is All About Trade-Offs

Strategy is all about planning while being aware of the business environment. Strategy is about being clear about what you do and what you don't do.

■ Create Marketing Space

Separate yourself from the competition. Make yourself different.

■ Focus On The Important

Know the difference between what is urgent and what is important. You must know what things are really important to you or to your business. And, if you know what is really important then you know what is less important and what is really unimportant. What excuses do you use to work on anything but the most important?

■ Seek First To Understand, And Then To Be Understood

You have two ears and two eyes but one mouth. When communicating, use them in that ratio. Listen, look and then speak. You need to understand where your audience is coming from before you can help them. To do any less is highly presumptuous.

■ Work *On*, Not *In* Your Business

When Ray Kroc started *McDonald's*, he never intended to work *in* the business cooking hamburgers; he always intended to work *on* growing the business. If you work *in* the business then you cannot work *on* the business. How much time do you need to spend working *on* rather than *in* the business?

■ Spend More Time Thinking And Less Time Doing

Spend more and more of your time thinking and less and less of your time doing. The role of the leader of an organisation is to spend time looking down on what is going on and take the broad view.

■ Less Is More – Simplify Everything

The simpler the concept, the more power it has. Use your time and your resources with care.

■ Ask Stupid Questions

Think the unthinkable and say the unsayable – how else will you be different from your competition?

■ Check The FOG Index

Consider that little gem that you are basing your decision on. Is it a fact, an opinion or a guess?

■ Stop Helping People – Let Them Fail

Only by making their own mistakes will your people learn.

■ Don't Shy Away From Passion

■ If Every Company Wants To Delight Its Customers, Then How Come We Don't Spend Most Of Our Customer Days Delighted?

■ Cut The Excuses – Just Do It

You can spend a minute, an hour or a day considering the implications of any of these one-liners for your business.

WHAT BRIGHT MARKETING IS NOT

Although the whole *BM* approach is a low cost one, it doesn't mean that it is in effect free. For a start, your time should always have a price on it – after all, it is your most valuable resource so spend/use it carefully.

You Will Need To Spend Money

When you do spend money, spend it well. You will need a professional looking logo, website – and as we say in the workshop – 'you must get the biggest bang for the buck that is possible'.

But It Is More Than Money

And the whole *Bright Marketing* thing is an entire waste of time and money if you don't do something as a result of it.

This book is all about action – make the decisions and take action!

THE BRIGHT MARKETING MANIFESTO

23 of the cardinal 'rules' of *Bright Marketing*

1. If there's a choice between being better or different then different wins every time
    – Ideally you should be different and better.

2. Why should people bother to buy from you when they can buy from the competition?
    – What makes you different from the rest?

3. Marketing is not a battle of the product; marketing is a battle for the mind of the customer
    – How will you win this battle?

4. You get known for what you do
    – So what is it that you are known for? Is it the right stuff?

5. Infect your customers and staff with your passion and excitement for your business
    – They are your ambassadors!

6. Selling is everything
    – Most businesses think their product/service is pretty cool so what's the problem? Go on a decent sales course, now.

7. Put your prices up, now
    – 95% of people do not buy on price, despite what they say.

8. What the customer thinks matters more than you can imagine
    – So do a customer survey, now.

9. Blow your customers away with your legendary service
   – Or they will leave you in droves.

10. Select your target customers and focus on them and
    what they want and need
    – ignore the rest.

11. Work the expert model
    – Become the leader rather than a follower in your
    field/marketplace.

12. Feel the fear and do it anyway
    – You won't die.

13. Don't compete on price
    – There's always someone out there who can do it cheaper
    than you and the last thing you want is a price war.

14. Understand and work your sales pipeline
    – How can you convert leads into clients faster?

15. Do the maths
    – Small changes in the right places have a massive impact.

16. Create a money and time budget for your marketing activity
    – And focus on results.

17. Spend time with weird people
    – You don't get great ideas staring at your computer
    screen.

18. Work the 80:20
    – Get effective by concentrating on the Law of the
    Vital Few and the Law of The Trivial Many – sack
    20/30/40/50% of your customers (and suppliers and
    staff!).

19. Ask for the business
    – If you are not asking for it then I am pretty sure that
    your competitors will be!

20. Make it easy for people to buy from you
    – Make it as easy as possible.

21. You are too much in love with your business
    – Get a grip on it!

22. Remove your self-limiting beliefs
    – What's holding you back?

23. Stop procrastinating
    – It's easier to ask for forgiveness than it is to ask for permission. Take action.

The Bright Marketing *Manifesto is a call to action; it encapsulates the philosophy and approach of Bright Marketers. 'Go For It!'*

GLOSSARY

30-Second Intro – *see One-Minute Intro*

80:20 – Pareto's Principle on the Law of the Vital Few and the Law of the Trivial Many

Ansoff Matrix – a matrix attributed to Igor Ansoff used for describing/ assessing marketing and strategy options

Audio Logo – *see One-Minute Intro*

BM – *Bright Marketing*

Brand – the messages that leak like radioactivity about your business

Break-Even Point – how many units you need to sell to cover your fixed and variable costs

Bright Marketing – an approach to marketing that depends on keeping things simple, effective and focused on the needs and wants of the customer

Bright Marketer/Marketeer – someone who follows the philosophy of *Bright Marketing*

Client – receives a service (a perishable non-storable item) and does not pay for it at the point of delivery (*see also Customer*)

Contribution – sales price less all costs, per unit

Culture – how we do things around here

Customer – someone who buys from you – normally just a one-off or short-term transaction for products that are paid for on the spot (*see also Client*) – also a generic term to cover the person receiving a product or service

Customer Acquisition Cost – how much it costs, on average, to acquire one new customer

Customer Lifetime Value – a way of considering the customer across their anticipated life as a customer of the company. CLV = (average number of years as a customer) x (Gross Profit per customer per year)

Customer Position – how you are positioned in the eyes of the customer

Differentiation – make yourself look different – differentiated marketing operates in several segments/sections of the market and designs separate offers for each

Education-based Marketing – using your marketing time and budget to educate and inform rather than to sell

Elevator Pitch/Statement – *see One-Minute Intro*

Endorsement – a testimonial or acknowledgement by a 'celebrity' who uses/enjoys your service

FastStrat – the Fast Strategy four-pager tool

FAQ – Frequently Asked Question

FiMO – a way of measuring performance to date of the business, standing for Finance, Marketing and Operations

FMCG – Fast Moving Consumer Good

Four Ps (or five or six) – the marketing industry's tired formula of Product, Place, Price, Product as well as (sometimes!!) People, Promotion, PR, Permanence, and anything else you can think of that begins with P!

GP (Gross Profit) – income less direct costs

Gross Margin – GP as a % of income

Inevitability Marketing – see your business as a 'money making' machine where you can choose how much to spend on acquiring clients with a relative certainty about the revenues and profits that this will generate

ITT – Invitation To Tender

KPI – Key Performance Indicator

Market Position – how you are positioned against the competition in the market

Ology – a proprietary point of view – your way, your system, for doing or seeing things

One-Minute Intro – a way to introduce yourself in less than a minute – not your job title but who your clients are, their problem, what you do to sort their problem and how they benefit

Point of View (PoV), Proprietary Point of View (PPoV) – *see ology*

Position – how you are placed or positioned

Positioner – someone who sets out to adopt a specific position

Positioning – the process of distinguishing a brand from its competitors so that it becomes a preferred brand in defined segments of the market – positioning is all about understanding the 'map' of where (and how and against whom) you are competing

PSF – Professional Service Firm, eg accountant, doctor, homeopath, consultant

Prospector – someone who is actively looking for prospects

RECOiL – a way of measuring capability/potential to grow business standing for Resources, Experience, Controls and Systems, Ideas and Innovation, Leadership

Referral – a contact/lead given by a colleague – it may lead to some work

Relationship Marketing – is about maximising long-term profitability through the intelligent use of information. The information is used to enhance and to create superior relationships with customers

Segment – a portion/section of people with a similar set of values or buying habits

Service – is not storable, is perishable, cannot be kept in inventory and once it has been delivered it cannot be used again

SMART Goals – goals, which are Stateable, Measurable, Attainable/Achievable, Realistic, Targetable/Timetable-able

Sneezer – someone who spreads an idea like a virus – a mover and shaker

Strategy – planning where you want to be while being aware of the outside environment

Tactics – low-level plans to make things happen

TBYB – Try Before You Buy

Testimonial – a letter or statement from an independent client that states how great they think you (or your services) are

Upsell – selling more to people than they originally wanted

USP – Unique Selling Point(s)/Proposition

Value-Added – the concept of adding value over and above the expected

Value Proposition – a statement that explains how you add value to the client

White Paper – a document that surveys the past and future of a market

WIIFM – What's In It For Me?

Word-of-Mouth Marketing – marketing that uses word-of-mouth to spread the word – ie not the standard marketing channels of TV, radio and press advertising

WSPB2BF – why should people bother to buy from you?

BIBLIOGRAPHY/ FURTHER READING

Beckwith, H. *Selling The Invisible.* Texere, 2002

Blanchard, KH & Bowles, S. *Raving Fans: Revolutionary Approach.* HarperCollins, 1998

Bly, RW. *Become A Recognised Authority.* Alpha, 2002

Craven, R. *Customer Is King.* Virgin Books, 2005

Craven, R. *Kick-Start Your Business.* Virgin Books, 2005

Cunningham, T. *eBig Business.* Virgin Books, 2002

Directors' Centre. *Selling Survey.* Directors' Centre, 2004

Edwards, P&S et al. *Getting Business to Come To You.* Tarcher, 1998

Gitomer, J. *The Sales Bible.* John Wiley & Sons, 2003

Godin, S. *Unleashing the Ideavirus.* Hyperion, 2001

Godin, S. *Permission Marketing.* Simon & Schuster, 1999

Godin, S. *Purple Cow.* Gardners Books, 2004

Hall, D. *Doing The Business.* Virgin Books, 2002

Harding, F. *Rain Making – Attracting New Clients.* Adams Media, 1994

Hayden, CJ. *Get Clients Now.* Amacom, 1999

Klaus, P. *Brag! The Art of Tooting...* Warner, 2003

LeBoeuf, M. *How to Win Customers and Keep them for Life.* Berkeley, 2000

Levinson, JC & McKenna, R. *Relationship Marketing – Successful...* Perseus, 1993

McLaughlin, MW. *Guerrilla Marketing For Consultants.* J Wiley & Sons, 2004

Maister, D. *Managing The PSF.* Free Press, 2003

Maister, D. *The Trusted Advisor.* Free Press, 2002

Misner, IR. *Seven Second Marketing.* Bard Press, 1996

Misner, IR. *World's Best Known Marketing Secret.* Bard Press, 1999

Ogilvy, D. *Ogilvy On Advertising.* Vintage, 1985

Peters, T. *Re-imagine.* Gardners Books, 2004

Peters, T. *The Circle Of Innovation.* Vintage, 1999

Ries A, and Trout J. *Positioning: The Battle For The Mind...* McGraw Hill, 2001

Sanders, T. *Love Is The Killer App.* Three Rivers Press, 2003

Seybold P. et al. *Customers.com: How to create a...* Times Books, 1998

Van Yoder, S. *Get Slightly Famous.* Bay Tree Publishing, 2003

www.bright-marketing.com
Website of the book – for articles, case studies, tools… This website contains a password protected area of free extras for readers of the book. (The password is 'bright'.)

www.directorscentre.com
The Directors' Centre

www.robertcraven.co.uk
Robert's own website

ABOUT THE AUTHOR

Robert Craven works with ambitious directors of fast-growing businesses who feel that they could be doing even better.

The Financial Times *describes him as 'the entrepreneurship guru'; Cranfield School of Management says he is 'the closest thing that growing businesses have to a modern day John Harvey Jones'.*

Robert set up the first of several businesses (restaurant, cafe, training company, sound studio) in his final year at university. He then spent five years running training and consultancy programmes for entrepreneurial businesses at *Warwick Business School.* Running his own consultancy since 1998, he is now one of the UK's best-known and sought-after speakers on entrepreneurship.

He is not full of theoretical rhetoric; he offers practical solutions – tangible business results. Robert's work on marketing and strategy has been widely published and acted upon by thousands of growing businesses.

His books *Kick-Start Your Business* and *Customer is King*, with Forewords by Sir Richard Branson, are both business best-sellers and have been described as *'truly inspirational'* by *The Independent.*

Robert's track record at helping businesses is very impressive. Add to this his broad experience at board level and you will understand how and why he uniquely adds value to all the businesses that he works with. Alongside his numerous speaking engagements, Robert also does consulting work for, and is personal mentor to, the leaders of a number of growing businesses in the UK.

Robert runs The Directors' Centre, the award-winning management consultancy company for growing businesses.

He lives in the countryside near Bath with his wonderful wife, two dogs and a cat – his three fabulous children have escaped to live their own lives!

For further details, Robert can be contacted at:
E: rc@robertcraven.co.uk   W: www.robertcraven.co.uk
T: +44 (0)1225 851044   Tw: @robert_craven

THE DIRECTORS' CENTRE

The Directors' Centre works with ambitious directors and owners of businesses who have concerns about the way their business is growing – they are growing too quickly or not quickly enough!

Clients work with us because we are challenging, honest and goading. The team knows how to grow a business – they have all been there and done it... which means that you get straightforward, no-nonsense solutions to your problems.

Areas of Expertise: Strategy, Marketing and Teams for growing businesses.

The 'ology':   A set of simple, yet powerful, tools that have been proven to work

Positioned as: Informal, practical and results-driven.

A Focus on: Entrepreneurship.

A Company led by: Robert Craven

So much more than just conferences and seminars...

Directors' Centre online Business Club offers tools, tips, techniques, videos and workbooks to grow your business www.directorscentre.co.uk

For further details about the Directors' Centre, contact:

E: office@directorscentre.com
W: www.directorscentre.com
T: +44 (0)1225 851044

Kick-Start Your Business – 100 days to a Leaner, Fitter Organisation

Author: Robert Craven
Foreword: Sir Richard Branson

This book is aimed at helping owner-managers and business advisers to maximise business potential. The emphasis is on practicality.

- Too much to do, too little time?
- Feel your business could do with a tune-up, but are too busy running it to sort out the problems?
- With the fast, proven techniques in this book, you can transform your workplace into a powerhouse.
- You won't find irrelevant management school theories here – just dozens of practical ways to turbo-charge any business.

Reviews

'Robert Craven's Kick-Start Your Business *covers an essential part of running a business… which will turn your business into a powerhouse by recovering some of the passion and nimbleness…. to make your business more effective and more profitable… the business in question often needs a boost – a kick-start to greater success in the future.'*
Sir Richard Branson

'Written in a no-nonsense style, Robert hasn't missed a trick.'
Start Your Own Business *magazine*

'If you want tips from the top, this book is for you. Inspirational stuff!'
The Independent. Featured in Top Ten Business Books

Product Details

- Paperback: 288 pages
- Publisher: Virgin Books
- ISBN: 0753509733
- Special Editions/Translations available in USA, India, Turkey, Brazil, Spain and China.

Customer is King – How To Exceed Their Expectations

Author: Robert Craven
Foreword: Sir Richard Branson

This practical hands-on book is for anyone running a business, or for professional marketers who have found that their methods don't work anymore.

- What happens when your customers try to buy from you?
- So, how do you separate yourself from the 'rest of the crowd'?
- With the fast, proven techniques in this book, you look at your business through your customer's eyes, understanding what they really want and, ultimately get them to buy more from you – and to buy again and again.

Reviews

'Robert Craven says that "your whole business hinges on what your customer gets from you". I wholeheartedly agree'
Sir Richard Branson

'...essential reading to the entrepreneur... Craven is one of the UK's best-known and sought-after speakers on entrepreneurship... anyone who has experienced his impactive presentations will know exactly why.'
Institute of Management Consultancy's *Professional Consultancy* magazine

Product Details

- Paperback: 288 pages
- Publisher: Virgin Books
- ISBN: 0753509687
- Special Editions/Translations available in USA, India, Turkey, Brazil, Spain and China.

Fulfil your potential

WHETHER IT'S BUSINESS OR PLEASURE, JOHN LEACH
REVEALS THE 10 STEPS TO A MORE SUCCESSFUL YOU

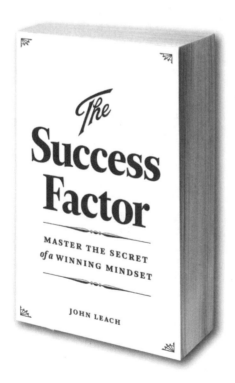

Visit www.crimsonpublishing.co.uk
to buy your copy and view the full business range